ON BECOMING WISE TOGETHER

THEOLOGICAL EDUCATION BETWEEN THE TIMES
Ted A. Smith, series editor

Theological Education between the Times gathers diverse groups of people for critical, theological conversations about the meanings and purposes of theological education in a time of deep change. The project is funded by the Lilly Endowment Inc.

ON BECOMING WISE TOGETHER

Learning and Leading in the City

Maria Liu Wong

WILLIAM B. EERDMANS PUBLISHING COMPANY

GRAND RAPIDS, MICHIGAN

Wm. B. Eerdmans Publishing Co.
4035 Park East Court SE, Grand Rapids, Michigan 49546
www.eerdmans.com

29 28 27 26 25 24 23   1 2 3 4 5 6 7

ISBN 978-0-8028-7906-6

Library of Congress Cataloging-in-Publication Data

A catalog record for this book is available from the Library of Congress.

For my dearest Tony, Joshua, Josiah, Immy, Mum, Dad, and Bethia

My City Seminary family and La Mesa TEBT

Contents

Acknowledgments

I am grateful for this opportunity to be at *la mesa* (the table) with friends and colleagues, sharing one part of a larger story of how God is at work in the world. I never would have imagined that waiting—in a line for COVID-19 testing that already stretched around the block in the dark before the sun rose—would be such an important theme in the work of theological education in this time between the times. But it is.

American songwriter Lincoln Brewster's "While I Wait" became something of a theme song these past three years, as I waited to recover from a snowboarding accident that led to my first-ever broken bone just before lockdown in New York City, and as we all wait for the many pandemics of COVID-19, racism, gun violence, and so much more to end. As we also wait for new ways of seeing and experiencing God to emerge, we are formed by the Spirit in the places to which God calls us, to the people and relationships with which we are privileged. The pandemic has made us rethink what we knew as "church," and what is possible.

This book would not have been finished without the support of my community at City Seminary, with whom I wrote this multilayered narrative of our lives together, this experiment in and expression of urban theological education. I am thankful for the support of Rev. Dr. Mark Gornik, my seminary director, who made time and space for me to finish this book. I am grateful for Minister Miriam, Pastor Adrienne, Bishop Vivian, Pastor Geomon, Pastor Adebisi, Pastor Huibing, Sarah, Rex, Kari Jo, Hannah, April, and so many others with whom I have shared my life over more than eighteen years.

Truly this book is my fourth child, born under the care of many midwives. First, there is *La Mesa* Theological Education between the Times (TEBT) project—Ted, Amos, Chloe, Colleen, Dan, Elizabeth, Hosffman, Keri, Lucila, Mark J., Mark Y., Rachelle, Tony, Uli, and Willie, with whom I shared space for critical dialogue, for writing and reading, for worship and theological formation.

Of those, I am particularly thankful for Amos and Elizabeth, whose insights and feedback in our writing trio were pivotal, especially in our early work together. Amos pointed me to the process of "becoming" a community of peace in the messiness of life together. He also encouraged me to make sure to include the voices of women leading in their own particular ways. Elizabeth, a pioneer in her own right as a Latina woman with particular wisdom and experience, fueled our conversations with her Nuyorican "fire." Our common experience of recovery due to stiff shoulders provided me with much strength and sustenance for this journey, and she still sends weekly texts to encourage and wish me "Shabbat Shalom."

Ted and Ulrike have been the most gracious and patient editors, making room for my starts and stops amid life here in the city. The last push was critical to getting the book done.

Then there are those who are mentioned in these pages—family, friends, colleagues, even those from whom I learned hard lessons around conflict and communication. Thank you for being part of the way I am being formed. To my mother, father, sister, and late grandmother Maa-Maa (嬤嬤 in Cantonese), this story is partly yours too. I would not be who I am without you.

Finally, and most important of all, thank you to my dearest Tony, Joshua, Siah, and Immy, for your prayers, nudges, jokes, warnings about watching too many K-dramas, and hugs; for sharing me with this manuscript over many years—yes, your fourth sibling.

I give thanks to God for the privilege of sharing this story of *imago Dei* in the city.

GRANDMA'S HOMEMADE DRESS

In Attire   Relationship: 👤   Group: City Seminary of New York

Grandma's homemade flower dress

I have kept this dress as a keepsake of "Maa-Maa", my late paternal grandmother (in Cantonese). It is a reminder of our family tradition of sewing our own clothes, one that has been shared by my grandmothers, aunts, mother, mother-in-law, and sister. The practice of making – whether out of necessity, economy, or enjoyment – has been formative to my life, and has taught me to use whatever is at hand, to be creative, and to cultivate my own style. Maa-Maa was born in Toisan, a village in southern China in the 1940s. After she moved to Hong Kong and married my grandfather, he went to the United Kingdom to find his fortune. She stayed in Hong Kong to take care of three young children, while he opened up a fish and chip shop, and sent money home. My grandmother also did some sewing to make ends meet. The family eventually reunited in the UK, and my parents were later married there. In 1981, my parents moved our family to New York. Maa-Maa joined us when Ye-Ye (paternal grandfather) passed away, and the tradition of sewing continued in our home together. Grandma had her own distinctive style, and added lots of pockets – inside and outside – to store her many knick-knacks. She had special places for money, her ID, and even snacks. She inspired and encouraged me to cultivate my own style. And I owe my love of creativity to her.

Place(s): China, Hong Kong, England, New York
Year: 1981

– ML

Relationship: 👤 Im/migrant

#CSNY_MinistryFellows1819A   #sewing   #Hong Kong

Grandma's Handmade Dress; "Our Story" online project screenshot, Tenement Museum (2018)

1

Waiting

"Tell each other a story about waiting."

Olga, my drama workshop partner, and I stroll through Socrates Sculpture Park on the edge of Long Island City in Queens, New York, considering this prompt. My mind wanders into unexpected territory. I wonder: Is this really the story I want to tell? With Olga listening attentively, I begin: "When I was a child . . ."

Half an hour later, it is our turn to share with the group. Olga and I lead the others to a grass clearing near some trees. The group forms a circle around her, and we watch as she flits from one person to the next in the circle. She moves gently back into the center and pauses for a moment before tracing her path to yet another person on the edge. Like a hummingbird, she is ever moving yet always finding her way back and forth to sanctuary.

This is her bodily interpretation of my story, the story of twelve years of my childhood.

The particular story I shared with her is one of me as a child waiting for hours on Sundays for my parents. I would start and end up in the first-floor lobby of our church, a nondenominational, immigrant Chinese church on the corner of Hester and Elizabeth Streets in Manhattan's Chinatown. Inevitably, I would go on a weekly adventure somewhere nearby before returning to the lobby to meet my family for the journey home. We attended this church almost every Sunday, from the time I was in first grade through the end of high school, commuting an hour or so from our home on Long Island.

Originally from Hong Kong, my parents moved at different times to the United Kingdom in the 1960s for education, marriage, work, the eventual births of my sister and me, and their broadcast ministry to overseas Chinese.

In the 1980s, our family moved to the suburbs of New York City, sponsored by a US defense engineering firm that hired my father. Here, my parents also served as local missionaries, reaching immigrant Chinese in restaurants, homes, and garment factories in the city through radio broadcasts and cassette tapes.

Often, they visited and spoke in different churches each week, sharing, encouraging, and praying with people not unlike my future in-laws, a seamstress and a chef. Some had come to New York City seeking a better life but lacked either time to attend or access to a traditional Sunday church service. Others, like my parents, had emigrated for higher education and stayed on for work. The overseas Chinese that gathered on those Sundays in Chinatown came from a range of socioeconomic backgrounds and cultures.

And each week, I was always waiting.

For hours on end, with my older sister Bethia and my paternal grandmother, Maa-Maa (嫲嫲), I waited for our parents to finish what seemed like endless meetings so we could make the long commute home together. These were the days before beepers and cell phones.

Here I am again in the church lobby, straining to hear my parents' voices, wondering if they are going up or coming down the stairs, and when they will finally be done and get the car to pick us up. Maa-Maa (嫲嫲) sits on a dull gray metal folding chair in the church lobby. She is wearing her sparkly blue-green dress that is featured in my Tenement Museum project story here, in this church, its shine and brightness obscured in a black-and-white photo, a dress that I have kept hung in a closet with me all these years. I would also hide behind her bedroom door to watch Chinese dramas and learn Hong Kong slang after school and on Saturdays. And it was with anticipation for both of us that she exchanged the rented videotapes we'd finished watching for a new batch every Sunday in Chinatown.

I smell a distinct whiff of the medicinal Maan-Gum-Yau (萬金油 Tiger Balm) that Maa-Maa (嫲嫲) applies generously to cure any and all ailments. I notice the small blue-speckled tiles glistening on the floor, the marble steps grayed from use, and, piled around my grandmother's feet, the ubiquitous red plastic bags of fresh wet green vegetables from the nearby street market. A long prickly green melon sticks out of a bag.

On those Sundays, I explore the streets near the church and local park and discover all the best places to hang out. I am oblivious to the dangers of streets designated by local gangs and somehow enjoy a markedly different experience from that of my husband, Tony, who grew up living in Chinatown but avoided being stopped to get recruited or beaten up in those same streets. We grow up in this place together yet apart, seeing the city with different eyes, our lives not intersecting until many years later when we attend our church's high school youth group together.

I slip out the front door of the church and, after playing volleyball in the park with friends, find my sister and go and explore the stationery stores for Sanrio mechanical pencils and erasers, or get a bolo-bao (菠蘿包 pineapple bun) from a Chinese bakery. Manna House Bakery on Mott Street is my favorite. I check in every now and then with Maa-Maa (嫲嫲) and see whether my parents have returned. Every time I appear, Maa-Maa's (嫲嫲) face brightens, reassured that I am okay. Then off I go again on yet another escapade around Chinatown, our second home, with its now familiar faces, places, and smells.

Such adventures and such waiting mark my childhood. They are my formation.

* * *

Perhaps you read this story and thought that my parents loved God sacrificially, and that our family bore the cost with understanding and patience. Or perhaps you thought that my parents could have made different arrangements rather than leave us to wait for hours each week. Maybe. But I wonder: Was this waiting part of God's plan to shape me into the person I am now? Through the act of waiting, did I—together with my sister and grandmother—somehow partner with my parents in missional vocation? In hindsight, I recognize that as a child I was already being formed for a vocation as an educator and theologian, in the home of missionary parents who believed that God's will was for us to do our best to bring others to him and to trust in his goodness for our family and for others.

Fast-forward a few decades, and my youthful impatience has been seasoned into another form of waiting, a way of becoming formed together with others for a life of ministry in the city. Now waiting has become a practice of trust, hope, and expectation that continues to shape me in relation to God, my parents, my sister, my late grandmother, and now my own family of five. It is an act of theologizing, of discerning how God is at work in our lives and in the world. And it is this waiting that cultivates in me curiosity and wonder, ongoing learning and transformation.

It is a process of becoming wise not to my own ways but to the ways of the Holy Spirit, engendering a sensitivity to what Asian American theologian Amos Yong calls a "pneumatological imagination."[1] He argues that the renewal of theological education for a "flat, connected and networked world can be found by reconsidering the primordial Pentecost outpouring of the Spirit." We need to ask: "What has the Spirit done? What might the Spirit be doing? What would the Spirit do? What would the Spirit wish for or empower us to do?"[2] So, I wait and bear witness to the Spirit's movement *in* and *with* a community grounded in time and place. It is a waiting that asks questions of life with critical intention, practical discernment, and Spirit-filled theological reflection. It is a waiting that invites the dynamic process of *becoming wise with others.*

This book reframes traditional Euro–North American conceptions of theological education by reflecting critically on my lived experience as a British-born Chinese–North American woman, a family member, an immigrant, an urban theological educator, a maker, a gallery curator, a community gardener, a Girl Scout troop leader, and a scholar. It is not limited to the context of formal institutions recognized as places where theological education happens, nor the content of a seminary curriculum as philosopher and theologian Friedrich Schleiermacher might have designed it in nineteenth-century Germany. It reimagines theological formation for the many together rather than the individual alone, and as happening in a wide range of times, spaces, and places.

I propose here that intercultural and communal understandings of theological teaching and learning suit the context of a complex and quickly changing urban world better than individualistic, rational Western habits of knowing. We are in the midst of a moment in which the reemergence of a model of collective wisdom is challenging the expert-knowledge approach that is bolstered by an information economy and capitalism. Traditional forms of theological education built out of a particular cultural and historical paradigm to educate individual, and usually male, ordained clergy are no longer relevant, accessible, nor sustainable; this is evidenced by multiple national studies on the decline of the North American church, diminishing student numbers, and increasing financial instability of theological institutions. The entire ecosystem of theological education is grappling with the need to reexamine systems and structures and innovate new "pathways to tomorrow."[3]

Now, *how and where we come to know* and *with whom we come to know* are as important as *what we know*. We are learning again how to learn. Rather than receiving inherited knowledge, we are expanding sources and means of understanding and being; *we are living theology as a verb.*

This collaborative approach to cultivating wisdom has some resonance with the early church. In Acts 1:12–14, when the apostles and others were sent back to Jerusalem to await direction after Christ's return to heaven, they gathered together, prayed, and waited. The Pentecost was a spiritual and physically embodied event that included the sound "of a violent wind" that came from heaven and "tongues of fire" that came to rest on each of them.[4] The filling of the Holy Spirit led to the powerful testimony of Christ's reality and good news, in every language of those present.

From there, a crucial decision was made in Acts 15 after much discussion and discernment through the Holy Spirit, namely, that the church need not be culturally homogeneous. Rather, the church was for the Jew *and* the gentile. *It was together that the church waited in order to become wise.*

In our own contemporary time of uncertainty and unraveling, we too are waiting, waiting for the wisdom needed for this turbulent age. We as a world Christian church can come together around what Latina theologian Elizabeth Conde-Frazier calls *la mesa*. This is not simply to redistribute power and resources from a historical center to the margins (presuming there even is a legitimate center) and to confront a legacy of structural and systemic racism in institutions and communities. It is an opportunity to witness a rearrangement of locations, a remapping of plural centers of power and margins of possibility.

The late African American writer bell hooks describes the margin as "a profound edge. Locating oneself there is difficult yet necessary. It is not a 'safe' place. One is always at risk. One needs a community of resistance."[5] By embracing the tension of writing out of the margin, from who and where I am, this work performs an alternative, aesthetic, oppositional act of becoming, of creating space to see differently and make meaning. It is a book I write to remember, to rehearse, and to map out what God has done in places where I come from, where I have been, and where I am going with others, with my "community of resistance." This is not simply nostalgia, as bell hooks points out; it is a "remembering that serves to illuminate and transform the present."[6] I take time to pause, reflect, and connect the dots of seemingly disparate stories that show how God is at work in my life.

In listening to and sharing stories of coming together around *la mesa*, we encounter the possibility to engage a complexity of kinds of knowledge and approaches to wisdom. Through such coming together as the diverse but unified body of Christ, we can enter a liminal space between what is familiar and what is unknown. This is true for theological education as it has been described, and for our world more broadly, in these times between the times.

The late Scottish missiologist Andrew F. Walls suggests that through such necessary coming together we are returning to an "Ephesian moment" in our day, a moment in which our global urban world reflects an even greater diversity than in the early days of the church of what it means to be "Christian." *The reality is that we need each other now more than ever.* "The very height of Christ's full stature is reached only by the coming together of the different cultural entities into the body of Christ. Only 'together,' not on our own, can we reach his full stature," notes Walls. This reimagining and reorientation take the form of the church flourishing in its diversity and *becoming God's shalom together* in the

6

city as family, friends, learners, and leaders. God's shalom is found in the reconciling of God's creation to right relationships with God, self, the other, and the natural and spiritual realms. If, as Walls suggests, "the purpose of theology is to make or clarify Christian choices," and if this attempt to think in a Christian way comes from within particular contexts and cultures, and in interaction with the Bible, then we are asking new questions every day. We are converting the material of life toward Christ through this Spirit-informed creative process that involves thinking, feeling, and acting. Yet will the church in all its diversity "demonstrate its unity by the interactive participation of all its culture-specific segments, the interactive participation that is to be expected in a functioning body? . . . Will the body of Christ be realized or fractured in this new Ephesian moment?"[7]

As it did in the early days of Acts when practices of radical hospitality challenged the intersectionally compounded boundaries of class, gender, law, and tradition, so today the physical and spiritual realization of the body of Christ has theological, social, and economic consequences. The implications are ever present in intensified moments of pandemic, protest, increased racism and violence, globalization, and climate change. The invitation is to embrace being a part of Christ's body while moving with others toward completion. In this movement, we need the generative work of the Holy Spirit to take action in us.

> Earth's creator, Everyday God,
> Loving Maker . . .
> Re-create us . . .

These phrases from British songwriter Bernadette Farrell's *Everyday God* point to the essence of how we, as the church, come into being: we are shaped and molded by the Spirit, our loving Maker. How? Through encountering, reflecting upon, and being transformed by the Holy Spirit in us. Remake and re-create us.

We see this in the practice of pilgrimage, of journeying together toward becoming wise and living out God's shalom, being

7

formed in our bodies as a diverse yet unified spiritual community. We work out this everyday theology grounded in particular times and places as individuals, as families, and as communities, yours and mine. For me and my family, it is in Socrates Sculpture Park in Queens in the 2020s; in New York's Chinatown in the 1980s; in Liverpool, England, in the 1960s; and in Hong Kong in the 1950s. When and where is such transformation happening for you?

As individuals and as a church, we all make choices and think in a Christian way in the places in which we are. We learn and lead as we seek the peace and prosperity of the places in which God has put us—in our families, schools, workplaces, civic spaces, and neighborhoods. We perform acts of compassion, care, and stewardship as we enact theology in the home and on the street. The goal of theological education, then, *is for God's people and creation to flourish, to reconcile brokenness, and to see grace and wholeness in families, churches, and communities in our world.* We search in faith for deeper meaning, to understand and respond to God's living presence as the Holy Spirit moves.

This work is full of struggle, lament, hope, celebration, and lessons of humility. In this formative process, the *telos*, or goal, of urban theological education shifts from being about the transfer of important knowledge from a teacher to a learner to being about *forming a wise community that daily embodies God's peace in the city and also points others to it.* Such a community bears witness to the movement of the Holy Spirit in our midst, and our need to respond with worship, repentance, reflection, prayer, and surrender.

By learning with and leading each other, family, friends, neighbors, and strangers have shaped my theological formation. This journey has been in the contexts of particular relationships, times, and places. It is a story of unconventional theological education that embraces formal, nonformal, and informal teaching and learning, one of diaspora movement and discoveries.

I begin at home with my parents, my sister, and my late grandmother. In its institutional forms, my journey winds its way from family and community to church and seminary, and from there into the street and public arena. Circles of influence overlap, and formation happens in expected as well as interstitial spaces and unanticipated places. Over time, I am being shaped as a learner, an educator, and a theologian in this everyday practice of doing "theology on the ground."

This story of communal learning is one that you don't hear often amid a dominant Eurocentric narrative of formal theological education. I give it voice with my own particular accent, rhythm, and cadence as a part of this book series. Turning up my usually quiet volume, I persist, speaking up and speaking out this story. My resilience is bolstered by those at *la mesa* who have welcomed, mentored, and nurtured me over the past few years. This circle of fellow educators, authors, and now friends in this project series has helped to expand my understanding of self, God, and others. Their insights into the ecology of theological education, articulated across North America and beyond, have shed light on the importance and timeliness of including my own perspective, mapped out alongside theirs and others.

Of course, many people besides me have brought their Christian faith to the city and have grown up shaped in transnational, cross-cultural, urban contexts. Theirs is also a diaspora story, though their origins may be rooted elsewhere in the world. They too are enacting theology in the day-to-day; they too are seeking God's peace together in, for, and with the city. In whatever place the Ephesian moment happens, the challenge is to reframe how to respond faithfully to this reality of the church's diversity and unity. I appreciate that others may have different perspectives and emphases in their experience of City Seminary and the practice of ministry. I cannot speak for them. But here, I tell my story as part of this developing narrative of theological education between the times.

* * *

Using critical autoethnography as a method, this book traces my physical journey from my biological family's roots in Asia and the student movements of the 1960s and 1970s to the United Kingdom, where my sister and I were born. It makes stops in various places around the world that have been the sites of my growth and transformation and returns to my present home, New York City. It also traces my experience of the emergence of a new, expanded, intercultural family of faith and learning.

City Seminary of New York, where I served as dean for twelve years and now serve as provost, is a grassroots urban theological learning community whose mission is to seek God's peace in the city through theological education. As members of this community, we live and journey and come around the table together as urban pilgrims; in so doing, we are in the flesh together becoming God's peace in our neighborhoods, city, and world. Together, we are the body of Christ in its many traditions—Apostolic, Baptist, Catholic, Episcopal, evangelical, independent, Methodist, Pentecostal, Presbyterian, nondenominational, and more. The seminary and the city are the spaces and contexts in which I have grown and continue to develop as an educator, friend, leader, and follower of Christ.

This book embeds my personal story in critical reflection on the times, the culture, and the contexts that have shaped this narrative and that of others whose stories have not yet been heard. It takes on a hopeful vision of what theological education can look like and be like in a global city where the church seeks to be missional and transformative as well as relevant and accessible. It asks hard questions and reflects on difficult lessons. But it also retains an undercurrent of faith and trust in God's creativity and ability to work with imperfect people in a broken world as together we seek wholeness in the kingdom work we do each day. It embraces a posture of curiosity and wonder at what is possible when God is at work in our lives.

I hope that this narrative, collection of images, and accompanying provocations shed light on ways and practices for seeking God's peace in the city (and other places) through the theological formation of leaders, families, and communities. While it can be helpful to others who have a similar vision, it is not something easily borrowed, replicated, and transferred. I have been asked more than once how the model of City Seminary of New York might look in another city. Our work has been born in a global city context and formed in a unique community of people whose stories have merged with God's story in a particular time and place. The shape and site of theological education in its institutional form must respond to what and who is there, and how the community came to be. Therefore, I urge you to look and listen carefully to your own context, as I have done to mine.

Writing this book has been both an act of worship and a pedagogical exercise. It is testimony, recounting how God has been at work in my life, in the places I have been formed. Yet it is also critical theological reflection; the cycles of action-reflection-celebration in themselves have become a process of discernment toward wisdom in and with community. I am grateful for those who have read these pages as they have evolved, and for what has changed as a result. I invite those who seek the same transformative possibilities for their cities to engage in their own process of map making, connecting the dots and creating meaning from the stories, people, and places that have shaped their experience of Christ in the city.

PAUSE AND REFLECT

- What points you to how God is at work in your city, in the everyday theology happening in your community? What images, people, places, practices, or stories come to mind?
- What are you waiting to see emerge as you find yourself during this season? What are you discovering about yourself, God, and others?
- How are waiting and wisdom interconnected for you? How do you see yourself being changed and transformed in and by a season of uncertainty and disorientation?
- In what ways are you willing to see, listen, and move with the Spirit's direction, grounded in your particular place and the particular people to whom God has called you?

CHAPTER 1

* * *

This book contains stories of how I have been shaped by others. I have had the privilege of journeying alongside a growing community of faithful citymakers at City Seminary of New York. I cannot name them all here, but I recall with profound gratitude colleagues, students, graduates, board members, friends, and donors who have supported City Seminary's vision and mission. We have given our loaves and fishes, and God has multiplied them beyond our imagination. We have grown in mutuality over time, learning lessons of faith and hope in our God with a heart for the city. The path has not been easy; there have been plenty of moments when we have been on our knees in prayer and surrender. At other times we have been humbled and encouraged by the faithfulness of the One who provides, the God who is good all the time.

So, I write this book to understand more deeply my own journey. I bear creative witness to what is more than meets the eye. It is a story that others continue to shape, interwoven and entangled in a testimony that will be retold and reinterpreted with a variety of accents and dialects whenever we testify how God has been working in our midst.

This faith journey takes us across continents in this book because place and life experience, as much as reflection and critical discourse, shape theology. I ask questions of God as teacher and learner, and bring knowledge and transformation through relationship to people and place and embodied acts. Because theological formation draws on the curriculum and experience of life, it is both intensely particular and individual, while also shared and communal.

My journey takes on the color and hue of context much as watercolor paint bleeds through paper, mixing shades and colors over time, saturating experience with the vitality of life. Such theological formation is also critical and mindful of the nuances of context, not idolizing constructs and systems that instead need to be questioned. So, this book is a personal testimony, a history lesson, a musing on place- and art-making, a cultural critique, a curriculum, a pedagogical practice, and an act of embodied resistance all in one.

* * *

A note about the autoethnographic method I use. Autoethnography is not memoir for the purpose of personal reflection. It is a research method that uses autobiographical data or observation to analyze, interpret, raise awareness of, and critique cultural assumptions. Autoethnography is an orientation for inquiry, using personal experience to understand the context of the political, social, and physical world in which self and community are shaped.[8]

This performative act of critical autoethnography takes multivocal, embodied form in me, a woman, British-born, with ethnic ties to Hong Kong and China, raised on the continuum of the suburbs and the city on the eastern coast of the United States. I am shaped by travel to five continents, living in multiple worlds, a code-switching, "third culture" kid with missionary parents living their faith through their own immigrant experience. I am an educator and scholar, an entrepreneur and institution builder, a maker and curator of spaces and experiences. I am a daughter, a sister, a wife, a friend, and a mother of three young people who challenge me to see and listen in new ways. You will hear this multivocality as I peel back layers of story and critique.

Borrowing from the work of British theologian Heather Walton, I frame this book as theological reflection in community as Christian practice. It is a way to speak out this story amid stories, inviting and compelling the reader to a transformative response. Walton notes that "our grasp of what is of utmost significance is as likely to be emotional and embodied as it is to be critical and rational . . . we are learning to value the wisdom that can come through deeply engaged practice."[9]

As such, this writing process—in conversation, in tears, and in laughter, with others at home, at work, and in community along the way—is in itself a part of doing theological reflection in and with the community. I lean into the wisdom of embodied practice. I invite readers to join in the conversation, to consider what role they might play in the present and future.

As a critical autoethnography, this personal and communal narrative interprets wider cultural trends as a way to analyze theological thought and practice. While it hopes for social transformation and change, this "joy-work," as African American theologian Willie Jennings describes it, also bears witness to the brokenness and fragility of our Christian testimony as human beings: faulty, redeemed, and forgiven. Culture is complex, socially constructed, historically situated, and inherently group-oriented, and this analysis attends to community both in person and in virtual form.

*　*　*

This opening chapter has introduced the importance of theological education, which I understand to include formal, informal, and nonformal learning. I have described the curriculum and context of theological reflection and formation as life itself, and have argued that theological education is for the many, not just the one. It has framed the methodology of critical autoethnography, and the way this book relates theological reflection with image and personal narrative from a doubly minoritized individual—an Asian diaspora woman in North America. In syncopated rhythm, it starts and moves along with image, story, reflection, provocation, and critique of the broader cultural context that will then be expanded over the next several chapters.

The second chapter focuses on the legacy of *family as a learning community*. I reflect on my family upbringing with missionary parents and the stream of visitors and volunteers that flowed through our open home to the basement recording studio. This informal theological education complemented my immigrant Chinese church formation at Oversea Chinese Mission (OCM), described in the opening story, where first-generation parents in the 1980s opted to hire a young white couple from Iowa with a heart for the Chinese to work with their second-generation children. These formative years at home, in church, in the city, and in other cultural contexts eventually led to seminary with my husband, Tony, a family affair as we brought our infant son Joshua to the very first class.

Family shaped and continues to influence my spiritual formation, theological reflection, and life practices. Every day, my choices as a wife, mother, daughter(-in-law), and sister reflect my beliefs and worldview. And family is also at the heart of my extended community at City Seminary of New York. Over the years, we have seen couples, siblings, adult children and retired parents, grandparents, cousins, church members, and colleagues become part of the continuum of lifelong learning that is happening in our midst. From high school youth in WE LEAD NYC youth seminary to retired seniors in our master of arts degree program in Ministry in the Global City, we are learning with and serving families.

In the third chapter, I describe the impact of *friends as theological educators*. Whereas other authors often describe friends in the context of dyads or pairs, I examine the impact of circles of friends, as Olga showed with her body in her hummingbird-like dance in this chapter's opening illustration. In the company of others, I see myself and them in new ways. I explore how friendship leads to theological formation in mutuality and community.

We have come to understand ourselves better at City Seminary through uncommon friendships shaped by the intentional diversity of our learning community. Faculty and students alike come from a range of cultures, races, countries of origin, church traditions, professions, life experiences, and socioeconomic and educational backgrounds. As Catholic scholar David Matzko McCarthy writes, "Through friendship we gain a sense of who we are and what the world is like—of the universe of the everyday."[10] Whatever metrics we use to determine success or impact, friendship over time is a key marker that learning and transformation are happening in community and in practice. Committing to sustain relationships with those who are different helps to mold who we are and how we live into the gospel.

In chapter 4, the focus shifts to *learning with others as holistic, interdisciplinary, and ongoing*. As a lifelong learner, my experience has been in communal endeavors. From formal schooling to short-term mission trips to Asia, Africa, and Latin America, my first job teaching elementary music in the South Bronx and then teaching English-language pedagogy in Ethiopia, learning with others has been part of the process. It has happened as theological formation in a doctoral cohort in an adult learning and leadership program, and as a part of a learning neighborhood where public faith means we live out being a good neighbor through the Walls-Ortiz Gallery in Harlem. Knowing and growing in the context of diversity require personal and communal accountability, and relationships are critical for shifting nonlearning to reflection and learning from experience.

As such, the pedagogy and philosophy of lifelong learning at City Seminary incorporate team teaching, cohort learning, artistic expression, multiple ways of knowing, diverse modalities of learning, action research, and reflexive praxis. We stress the ways that theological formation is not just a course of study for a particular time but growth that takes place throughout a person's entire life. Lifelong learning is life-wide, across all parts of life, and life-deep, engaging our deepest questions and longings. And particularly in the context of the pandemic, we are reminded that bodies and places matter.

Chapter 5 explores *leading in dynamic practice with others*. Leading involves movement, alone or with others, into and out of multiple possible arenas of influence, what I describe as dancing into the centers of a spiral labyrinth with multiple centers. I have learned this through my family, from generations of Asian American women leaders, and with thirteen racial ethnic minority women leaders in global theological education in Africa, Asia, and North America in my doctoral research.

This impacts how I lead with others at City Seminary. Whether creating spaces for and with pastors and ministry leaders, praying through New York City neighborhood by neighborhood, or walking with young people as they wrestle with critical questions of faith and life in the city—we learn and lead together. As these stories unpack what it means to lead, we see time and again that it is the "priesthood of all believers" to which 1 Peter 2:5–9 points us.

For whom is theological education, and who leads in the work of theological education? It is for and by children, youth, young adults, parents, aunts, uncles, grandparents, families, friends, neighbors, churches, and communities; we learn and lead with each other.

Finally, in chapter 6, I close with *becoming wise in community*, considering how the table and the pilgrim journey enable us to embody our witness of the "living mystery" of the incarnational gospel of Jesus Christ. This happens in the slow, prayerful, and persistent work of building intercultural, intergenerational relationships that we hope will move us as a church, society, nation, and world toward God's justice and radical peace. As the long history of anti-Asian hate and violence in this country continues to escalate alongside the growing #BlackLivesMatter movement and resistance to systemic and structural racism, I find the need to speak up compelling and urgent. How *do* I answer the questions my children, my students, and my neighbors ask? What *should* we be doing?

Mirroring the earlier chapters, I explore how becoming as a process involves family, friends, learning, and leading. I read Proverbs 31:10–31, the poem of the "valiant woman," through an Asian diaspora woman's lens, in light of the stories I have shared. I illustrate how *phronesis*, or the practical wisdom of knowing how to discern, takes form in the witness of my husband in a season of deepening in his vocational journey. I reflect on the legacy of mentors and friends in our seminary community. And I close with reflections on learning what it means to be leaderful in my growing civic engagement with the Asian American Pacific Islander community in New York City.

I return to the liminal space, the betwixt and between, the process of being formed in and over time—both *chronos* in its sequential sense and *kairos* as the opportune moment. On our knees, praying a prayer of lament and healing, we encounter self, God, and others. We begin again, waiting around the table in order to become wise.

AN INVITATION

bell hooks writes:

> This is an intervention. A message from that space in the margin that is a site of creativity and power, that inclusive space where we recover ourselves, where we move in solidarity to erase the category colonized/colonizer. Marginality as site of resistance. Enter that space. Let us meet you. Enter that space. We greet you as Liberators.
>
> Spaces can be real and imagined. Spaces can tell stories and unfold histories. Spaces can be interrupted, appropriated, and transformed through artistic and literary practice.[11]

Likewise, I invite you into this space of creativity, image, and story, as readers from different spheres of life. Whether you are clergy or lay leader, scholar or practitioner, theologian or educator, artist or activist, have another role entirely or hold multiple roles, I welcome you to ask questions of what I lay bare in these pages.

Are you trying to open up conversations about alternative perspectives, or are you simply tired of representing "the other"? Consider these provocations as you reflect on how you make sense of what and how these stories make you see and feel. Talk about them to someone. Show what they look like in the form of an image, gesture, color, or even a taste. How might that change how you see or experience what you have shared?

- What possibilities for change emerge from the stories that I tell?
- What stories of your own have led to transformation?

- What hope do you hold for the future of theological education between the times?

Images punctuate the beginning of each chapter and emerge juxtaposed alongside stories and reflection. These images are taken from my bedroom windowsill, from my living room, and from boxes of treasures saved in my closet, moved from one apartment to the next. They are the products of a lifetime of remembering, of claiming the stories that God has told in my life, of naming how I have learned and what I am still learning. They are a collection of artifacts that show what theological education for me has been and what it can be. They are a different source of knowledge and wisdom taken from life.

Drawing from visual-thinking strategies to imagine and catalyze conversations at City Seminary, I invite you to consider what artifacts or images hold meaning for you as you consider how *you* have been formed in faith for ministry. As you examine them, ask yourself these questions:

- What do you see? What else do you see? What about it makes you think that?
- What is this object or image? What does it look like? What senses are evoked by the memories of this object? Where did it come from? Who and what is involved? How does it make you feel? Why? How does it help you tell and understand your story?
- What testimony of God's work in your life and in the world can you share with others? How have you come to know this?

The Anglo-Irish poet David Whyte writes:

Courage is the measure of our heartfelt participation with life, with another, with a community, a work; a future. To be courageous is not necessarily to go anywhere or do anything except to make conscious those things we already feel deeply and then to live through the unending vulnerabilities of those consequences.

19

To be courageous is to seat our feelings deeply in the body and in the world: to live up to and into the necessities of relationships that often already exist, with things we find we already care deeply about: with a person, a future, a possibility in society, or with an unknown that begs us on and always has begged us on.[12]

It has taken a lot of effort for us to face this present moment, to be honest with where and how we have arrived, and to look squarely at the future. We wait in this in-between time, needing to go deeper into what has been and what is before us. To what extent do you have the courage to trust, hope, and live in faithful anticipation of what is to come?

* * *

Now I live only fifteen minutes from that street corner where as a child I waited. After high school, I moved into the city and now raise my three children with my husband on the Lower East Side in Manhattan. Though I no longer attend my childhood church, I remain closely connected to the community in which I was formed.

We are waiting for life to resume some sense of normalcy, perhaps not what was but what will be a safer, more just version of city and global living. We want to live in our home, in a neighborhood where my elderly in-laws are not afraid to walk the streets for fear of being attacked merely because of what we look like and who others perceive we are, where we don't need to carry a personal alarm and pepper spray.

My children are also learning this lesson of waiting, of becoming God's peace in our neighborhood and city. Their story is local to this global city, the next chapter in our family legacy. This story is heightened by the COVID-19 pandemic and what will follow. We are all literally waiting in this pandemic portal from the old to the new, for a way of life now marked ever more so by the interconnectedness of our bodies and breath. The news. The numbers. The stories. The reopening. The reclosing. The protests. The fake news. The next wave. The vaccine distribution. The Delta variant. The booster. The Omicron variant. The attacks. The rallies. BA.2, 3, 4, and 5. Monkeypox. Polio. What's next?

My children live in a much more diverse community than the one in which I grew up as a child. This is intentional. In prepandemic times, they joined me up at the seminary in Harlem on Saturdays or school holidays, not just waiting for me to finish my meetings but becoming a part of the seminary community themselves. They took part in gallery activities, sharing their ideas about the community through artwork in the makerspace or in a Zoom art-making workshop. They walked and prayed with me in neighborhoods around the city.

Our home is an extension of the learning space, a space in which we once hosted, and hope to host again in the future, staff and students for meals, meetings, and fellowship. We embody God's peace and, at times, much laughter, as a larger "family" in our New York City apartment.

As they interact with Po-Po (婆婆 maternal grandmother) and sometimes Gong-Gong (公公 maternal grandfather) in Hong Kong over Skype weekly on Saturday evenings, my children's transcontinental theological formation continues. Sometimes the technical difficulties mean they can't hear or see each other, and they have to wait—again—until things are sorted out and they can continue their devotions. Recently, we laughed over a compilation of "Are you ready for Skype, Po-Po (婆婆)?" clips my oldest son had compiled over the years into a video.

And the story comes full circle: now it is me and my parents who are waiting, waiting for my children to live into their own faith as they are formed as the next generation of Christian believers. It is my hope that one day they will read this and remember for what and for whom we are waiting. We await the coming of Hope in its completeness in a time that has been darkened by the shadow of death, violence, and loss. It is for this future—their future—that I write this book.

Let this story be one that bears fruit as we seek God's wisdom and healing, and become God's peace in the city together.

"Home" installation inspired by artists Do Ho Suh and Mei Kazama; Brooklyn Museum of Art teaching workshop; photo by author (2020)

Family

Do you have time to remember?

"8:30 a.m. Bible study." As I head to the bathroom, my younger son, Josiah, eight years old, stops me in the apartment hallway and hands me a slip of paper with these words written on it. The kids are home from school because it is Yom Kippur. We live in New York City, where Jewish holidays are part of the public school calendar. I have just come back from a morning run, and Tony is getting ready for work.

"What is this?"

"We're having Bible study, home church. In our room. But you can't come in yet. Wait in the hallway."

Promptly at 8:30 a.m., my husband, Tony, and I knock on the door of the boys' bedroom. Josiah is standing in front of the far window with his dog-eared devotional Bible and some papers nestled on a music stand. A two-part handwritten sign, *"WELCOME TO . . . BIBLE STUDY,"* is taped to the side of the bunk bed. On the wall above the bottom bunk, more signs are hung up: *"GOD MADE EVERYTHING"*; *"ARE [*sic*] GOD IS SO GREAT. So strong and so mighty . . ."*; *"WORSHIP GOD."*

His thirteen-year-old brother, Joshua, is sitting on a low stool in the closet, a laptop precariously balanced on his long legs, music cued to a YouTube video of Chris Tomlin's *"Here I Am to Worship."* And Immy, our youngest child at five, greets us in her pajamas and passes out printed song sheets for worship.

"Please sit down. We're going to start now."

Two black plastic folding chairs have been set up in the middle of the room facing Josiah's podium. We settle in and get comfortable. The service begins.

"Good morning, everyone. Welcome to church."

Josiah starts with a short announcement and prayer, and music from the closet signals that it is time for worship. After we sing two songs, he reads a passage from Proverbs and a reflection from his devotional book. This is the book that Po-Po (婆婆) has given him for their weekly devotions. We pray together, and then it is time for "coffee hour" in the dining room.

This is the first of a series of "home church" sessions led by the three siblings. Though such sessions are not as frequent now that the three have grown into adolescence and young adulthood, home and church—in these pandemic times—continue to overlap and blend together. In the midst of the reopening transition, the kids had Zoom sessions for Sunday school and youth group. During dinner, we had evening worship with YouTube. It was not quite the same as "home church," but I am grateful we had time set aside to worship together.

As a parent, I hope and pray that home will always be a part of where and how we experience God together, and that I will continue to be led by my children into worship. At the Chinese church of our youth, Tony and I were formed in a nondenominational tradition. We have given our children the freedom to choose a "believer's baptism." Our youngest asked to be baptized, but the boys have not yet. I wait to see how God will meet my sons in their stories of formation. Growing up as second-generation missionary, or ministry, kids (MKs), they can find family complicated. But I wait and hope.

* * *

The process of theological and spiritual formation at home is a legacy of faith intertwined with *family as a learning community*. It is the subject and site of learning and practice inside and outside of the home. Daily rhythms of life, the everyday practices of who we are, the roles we play within our families, and the spaces we inhabit: these shape our theological thinking and how we testify with our bodies. Our choices and habits form us into beings that, while imperfect and often impatient, together seek to embody

God's wholeness and goodness. We do theology together in our homes and wherever we are—as a family.

This chapter presents a series of stories that shed light on the significance of multiple dimensions of family in the arc of spiritual and theological formation. My version of "family" includes multiple generations, near and far away, and is not limited to biological ties. The family is a place and context where the Holy Spirit works on earth, as generations teach and learn from and with each other. Family is the space where single and married people, young and old, individuals connected by faith or blood, are integral to what it means to be formed in Christ together. And while "family" and "home" can be contested spaces where theological malformation can happen, here I focus on helpful and hopeful ways that they contribute to theological formation and education.

I reflect first on "home" as a space to care for self and other. Then I share about my family upbringing as a local-global MK and its implications on my parenting. I describe my own turning point of faith on a short-term mission trip to Guatemala and how I shared it with my son years later. I then consider the nuances of family formation as spiritual and extended families, in the context of my formal seminary experience and the participation of family. I conclude with the ways in which theological education of family is lived out at City Seminary. This happens in the student and faculty body, and in our efforts to engage the generations through our WE LEAD NYC youth seminary and research. Family shapes spiritual and theological thinking as well as life practices. So, theological education and transformation in this context are intended for the many as well as for the individual.

* * *

I have tucked the "skidule" from an early "home church" gathering into the back pocket of a journal, pictured in the opening image of this chapter. This photograph captures a vision of "home," a mini-installation of a care space evoking family, memory, and formative experiences. I took it during an on-

line Brooklyn Museum of Art teachers' workshop with Japanese American artist Mei Kazama last year.

Inspired by the work of Korean artist Do Ho Suh, whose life-sized re-creations of places where he lived engage with themes of migration and cultural displacement, we are asked to draw or write about what it means to take care of ourselves and others during these pandemic times.

"Checking in on neighbors. Limiting or turning off the news. Zoom meet-ups. Cooking extra meals for others. Going for a walk."

Then we consider: What memories, people, spaces, or objects come to mind?

"A candle. Good food. The living room sofa. FaceTime. Family and friends."

We discuss resources and strategies to support students in feeling cared for in their homes and in our classes. I think about the stresses and strains of adult students who are juggling parenting, work, and other responsibilities.

We brainstorm how to create a space in our homes to remind us to pause and take care of ourselves. For twenty minutes, we work off-screen to collect and arrange objects—scraps of fabric, colorful paper, bowls, things we have around the house, tape, string, and thumbtacks to create this installation. I have plenty to work with.

A dark brown devil's head water chestnut from a family kayaking trip on the Hudson River, a white pebble from a hike at Bear Mountain, a shell from a trip to Jones Beach, and a handwritten note to myself to pause and rest—all these accompany my journal. This journal documents memories of people and places important to me.

A cream-colored soapstone bowl with swirls of gray from Kenya holds a folded pink-colored crane my daughter gave me and a ball of gray-blue acrylic yarn from our crocheted flower installation for the Fresh Oils Community Garden entrance gate in Harlem, the current expression of the Walls-Ortiz Gallery. Next to it, I place a dark brown clay sculpture of a family of five from a street market in South Africa and a light-blue ceramic candlestick holder discovered at a craft shop on my honeymoon in Sweden.

A small pillow encased in a blue and gold African print fabric, purchased from a Nigerian student-entrepreneur at a pop-up artisan fair we hosted at the gallery, leans against the wall. And to the left, I place a plant with bright orange flowers and grassy green leaves. All these are displayed on top of a bright multicolored woven wool blanket from Guatemala, kept from my first life-changing short-term mission trip.

These objects represent a memory, a place, an experience with or without people. Each one captures a relationship that reminds me of care—for self, for others, and for God, and how I have been formed by that care. The installation is now replaced by a monitor and a table for my WFH (work from home) office. But the memories continue to illuminate and transform the present.

PAUSE AND REFLECT

- What does it mean to care for yourself and others? What does "community care" look like? Take some time to collect and gather together your own "home" installation. Think about the ways this sacred space invites you to pause and consider how God has been at work in your life.
- Do you have time to remember?

* * *

"Oh, how cute! Say that again!"

"Banana (buh-naa-na). Tomato (tu-maa-toe)."

"Where did you say you were from again? England? I thought you and your family came from China."

Actually, not all Chinese people are born in China. We've been traveling the world for centuries.

"Your English is so good."

That would be because English is my first language.

When my sister and I arrive in the suburbs of New York City, she is seven and I am five. One day I come home from school, according to what my father recalls, and ask: "How come I don't have yellow hair and blue eyes?"

He pauses. His eyes open wider. He exclaims: "What? We are Chinese!"

* * *

I came to New York as an immigrant from the United Kingdom. When my sister and I, with our Chinese faces, opened our mouths and spoke with British accents, there were quizzical looks and raised eyebrows in our small town on Long Island where the population was predominantly white Catholic or Jewish.

My family's journey to and from the United Kingdom began with my paternal grandfather, Ye-Ye (爺爺). In the 1950s, he moved to Wallasey in northwest England, to make a living running a fish-and-chips shop. This was years before my grandmother, my father, and his two younger sisters joined him. They almost moved to the United States when my father was accepted into a medical program, but his application for a student visa was denied. From what I've been told, it was either because he wanted to be a medical missionary or because his extended family already lived in the United States and the officials at the US embassy were afraid he would not return.

My grandparents and their family settled instead in England, and my father began his studies in engineering at the University of Liverpool. A few years later, my mother relocated from Hong Kong to join him. They met in Hong Kong earlier while serving together in a summer gospel camp, and friendship blossomed into marriage. After graduate school in Manchester, my father went to work for British Telecom and invented a technical device that was patented. It was during the years of the Cold War, and an American defense firm reached out to recruit him. Our family, which had relocated by then to southeast England, where my sister and I were born, moved to the United States.

In the midst of all this, my parents were also missionaries. They had been formed by the fervor of student campus movements in Hong Kong in the 1950s and 1960s.[1] They founded a broadcasting ministry using cassette tapes color-coded by category (evangelism, testimony, discipleship, worship, etc.) to evangelize to overseas Chinese living in London and beyond. They took very much to heart the spirit of Matthew 28:19–20 to "go and make disciples of all nations, baptizing them in the name of the Father and of the Son and of the Holy Spirit, and teaching them to obey everything I have commanded you."

My parents converted our London home into a makeshift studio. They used the kitchen as the recording room and the sitting room as the control room for my father's hi-fi sound system, bought secondhand at a professional outlet. They hung up a sleeping bag as a sound buffer. My father managed the technical aspects, and my mother wrote scripts and produced the programs.

After our move to the United States, they built a basement studio in our house on Long Island and continued the work. By day, my father worked as an engineer in a Long Island defense firm. By night and on weekends, he and my mother recorded evangelistic and discipleship programs in ten or so Chinese dialects in our basement. When they arrived in New York, my parents connected with the network of immigrant Chinese in the city and the surrounding suburbs who were working in and beyond local churches with a vision to serve their cultural community.

A mélange of transnational Chinese people visited and stayed in our home to record—Spanish-speaking Chinese missionaries from Latin America, visitors with Aussie accents, pastors and church workers from Malaysia, Singapore, Hong Kong, China, and Taiwan. The programs were broadcast over the public address system of garment factories, distributed to restaurant workers, shared with people who could not attend worship on Sundays, and given to grandparents (whose grandchildren might have difficulty communicating with them) to listen in their home language.

Growing up in the midst of the comings and goings in our home, my sister and I became "third culture" kids, belonging neither entirely to one nor another culture. We were constantly negotiating our hybrid identities as British and Chinese immigrants in a North American, predominantly white suburb while spending weekends in Manhattan. In Chinatown, we looked Chinese, but we were suburban, not city, kids. We were jook-sing (竹升), which literally translates as "bamboo pole," and refers to a compartmentalized hollow bamboo plant stem in which water that enters in one end does not necessarily flow out the other end. It is a term used to describe second-generation Chinese Americans, who don't speak Chinese fluently or understand Chinese culture in the same way as their parents.

Our parents tried to help us retain their home language. They made us respond to them in Cantonese if they spoke Cantonese to us, and in English if they spoke English. So, we had to negotiate constantly what we were hearing and saying, with Chinese language being very much contextual and relational, and English much more direct. Our filters for life outside the home were complicated by these linguistic and cultural dynamics. We learned to code-switch, reading and listening carefully to the variety of contexts we encountered.

We were double minorities, missionary kids with limited means growing up in an affluent town on Long Island. My parents had chosen this school district so that my sister and I could continue in the same grade we had started in the United Kingdom. We were a year younger than everyone else in our classes. We were shorter, smaller, and spoke with different accents. I was called "Shrimp" for as long as I can remember.

It was a financial stretch for us living on my father's daytime income, as my parents' ministry was supported by faith and financial donations. While our classmates' first cars in high school were Lexuses and Infinitis, we wore hand-me-down clothes and walked to school and to the train station for trips to the city. We mowed the lawn, trimmed the hedges, raked the leaves, and shoveled the snow ourselves instead of hiring a landscaping company. We were the "scholarship" kids in music camp and Saturday art school.

We knew we were different because at the yearly international potluck celebration in elementary school only a handful of us wore traditional cultural outfits and brought in dumplings, kimbap, noodles, and fried rice, or curry and naan. By the time we were in middle school, there were more families from India, Persia, and Korea, including some who moved east from Flushing, Queens, in search of better schools and bigger houses.

Yet we lived full lives, maneuvering along the continuum between our home, New York City, and the world, forming character, curiosity, and openness to a sense of purpose and possibility. Korean American scholar Deborah Hearn Gin writes about the strength of the Moabite Ruth's multivocality as a foreigner in a new land, learning how to leverage her different identities and roles as widow, daughter-in-law, and caretaker.[2] This resonates with how we were trying to make sense of who we were and how we were to be in a range of spaces and places. We learned this was a gift and a strength, not a liability. We could use difference as a standpoint to learn.

As we grew older, my sister and I began to discern our own callings. We found ways to integrate our Christian faith and vocation. She became an architect and communications strategist. I became an educator-scholar and curator, bringing together disciplines and life experiences in ways I could not have foreseen. Our journeys overlapped as she worked alongside my colleague Mark and me from early on, strategizing how to translate the story of City Seminary through graphic design and other means.

Ironically, after not wanting to end up walking the same path as my parents, I followed them in a different way: with others, I shared in the work of building an urban intercultural theological community grounded in New York City. Instead of bridging distance through tapes, radio, or Internet broadcasts, my ministry was formed very much in the face-to-face, embodied interaction of the local church.

My parents continued their broadcast ministry through the Internet in Asia after my sister and I graduated from college. In fact, my father began the transition back to Asia while I was still in high school. He ended up working for two years in Hong Kong while my mother took care of us in New York and did a master's degree in communications at a local university.

They expanded their work over the years using digital audio players, shortwave radio, and Internet broadcast. Because they spent most of their lives on the frontlines of ministry, my parents never had the time or space for formal theological education. My mother tried twice but was unable to complete a doctoral program in missiology—not through any lack of intellect (she had, after all, graduated from the prestigious Hong Kong University), but because the pressure to serve and continue in the daily work of ministry made it difficult for her to take time for reading, reflecting, and writing. Instead of academic papers, she spent her time writing scripts and prayer newsletters. She could have brought a wealth of experience and insight to the classroom if she had the opportunity to finish her formal theological education.

I wonder sometimes how my parents experienced their entrepreneurial faith as missionaries in our immigrant Chinese community. They seemed confident in God, who made the impossible possible and who made miracles happen. But I can imagine how difficult it might have been for my mother as a woman of her generation, gifted in ministry leadership but limited in opportunities because of gendered cultural and denominational expectations. If she—a gifted speaker—had been a man, would the ministry have grown in a different direction? My father, whom my mother has helped to plan and write out his talking points for years, was definitely the technically gifted partner in the ministry. How would their partnership have evolved over the years if their cultural context had not been so conservative?

My father also juggled work in an American engineering firm as an immigrant British Chinese man trying to adjust to a new culture while experiencing racism and discrimination. There was one very scary time when my mother discovered him at his office not feeling well because of a stomach ulcer, presumably from stress. Later he would have a heart attack, during my first year out of college. These were physical repercussions as he tried to be a good father and a provider for our family while following and obeying God's call into ministry with my mother.

My parents are now in the twilight chapter of life—though my father would like to think he is still in his prime and though he operates as if he is! In his late seventies, he wants to keep going and never retire. He'll stop when he drops. Literally. I wonder how much our family has become victim to cultural ideals or idols that call us to work harder and harder. The Protestant mission ethic and Chinese culture tell us that to suffer and to persist is to be faithful, while to rest is to be idle. It could also be the legacy of a working-class childhood and the desire to provide for his family that pushes him.

My mother has been hoping to write the story of how they fit into a movement of Chinese Christian mission that evolved over the last several decades. This mission came out of theological formation that did not happen in a classroom but in a basement studio, in garment factories, in restaurants, and in people's homes—in our home and with our family.

There are seasons in life that mark our journeys, milestones at which we recall God's hand guiding us along the way. Even as the COVID-19 pandemic turned things upside down, the protests in Hong Kong and shifts in the political situation there halted my parents' weekend commutes to and from China and led to a more permanent stay in Hong Kong. Health concerns added to the complexity of slowing down and responding to change after a lifetime of ongoing ministry.

As their adult daughter, I face the challenge of knowing how to honor and respect the wisdom of my elders in this third chapter of their lives. I wrestle with how to encourage them into a season of reflection, remembering, and celebration—living into their vocation in a different way. This waiting for answers forms us theologically in the midst of a new set of questions. Care takes shape in a different form, with restrictions on physical travel juxtaposed with daily access through Skype and email.

The joy-work I am doing in this book and at the seminary is about taking the time to remember and to document. I realize more and more how critical it is to keep track of and share the stories of ministry on the frontlines before it becomes the memory of a few, not archived in a form that honors the significance it has for the global church. There are many whose faithful ministry over the years is unknown or untold.

The legacy of my parents' work and of their practices of hospitality and faith affects my own family—my husband and three children—as this chapter's opening story depicts. I am a mother aware of how my choices affect my children and their theological formation. In our close-knit immigrant Chinese community growing up, there were always eyes watching and ears listening. I heard from my parents about aunts' or uncles' comments about with whom or how I was spending my time, especially if a boy was involved. And then there were the comparisons with so-and-so. At some point, I concluded as a teenager that if this was what it meant to be an adult in a church, I did not particularly care for it. I also witnessed friends who were PKs (preachers' kids) and MKs rejecting their childhood faith because of this.

On the other hand, there were also children who followed in their parents' footsteps, leading the choir or heading the children's ministry. The pastor's family was involved in all aspects of ministry, or at least that was the expectation. The pastor's wife had a role to play. It was a "two-for-one" deal.

While my parents were not pastors, they were ministry leaders with expectations that their children would be role models for others. In this conservative evangelical Chinese world, rock 'n' roll was the devil's music and our Catholic friends needed to be "born again" or go to hell. So, I grew up with classical music and public radio (and occasional new wave music with friends), and to this day, I can't really remember the names or lyrics of popular songs or groups. Karaoke is not my thing.

Because our home was open at all times to volunteers, pastors, and ministry leaders, we had to be on our best behavior and ready to serve. Perhaps I grew busy with my own activities at school and elsewhere in order to find a reason *not* to have to fold brochures or edit newsletters. Sometimes I just wanted to be like everyone else around me. It was exhausting to constantly make sense of the two very different worlds, one inside and one outside of our home.

As it turned out, among the very people my parents sought to reach—immigrant Chinese making a living in garment factories and restaurants—were my future in-laws. My mother-in-law worked as a seamstress in a garment factory in Chinatown, while my father-in-law worked as a chef in Chinese restaurants in New

Jersey and Connecticut, and later at the local senior center in Manhattan's Chinatown. My life intersected with theirs when I met their son Tony in our church high school youth group. He jokes that he was the answer to my parents' prayers—that I find a good Chinese boy from the same home region in China. This way I could communicate with his parents, who speak Toisan (台山話) and Cantonese (廣東話), which I had learned at home from Maa-Maa (嫲嫲) when she came to live with us. God has a sense of humor and a plan in place. Always.

The balance of two parents with contrasting familial home experiences, in this case, has helped us care for our family. Together my husband and I have many choices to make about how much to incorporate our children into seminary life, how to maintain healthy boundaries, and how to cultivate their spiritual formation. When we talk these things through at the dinner table, we theologize together with them. We are learning together and becoming formed by and with each other, in order to live into a lifetime of ministry with breathing space for the Spirit.

* * *

"Gracias!"

I am fifteen years old, and our church's short-term mission group has just finished doing a puppet show in a Catholic mission school for children living near the Guatemala City garbage dump. I am the second youngest in the group, and this is my first trip. We give out lollipops and stickers to the children, and chat with them in our broken Spanish. We swat away flies attracted by the sticky sweetness of the candy on kids' faces. Finally, we pack up our things and get ready to leave.

I walk around the corner from the school and stop midstep.

Huge black birds in a blue-gray sky circle above the largest mounds of garbage I have ever seen, swooping down every so often when they spy something to eat. There are so many mountains, speckled throughout with color and just about everything one can imagine. So many birds. And then in the midst of it all, I see something else move.

It is a person.

Actually, it is people climbing up and down, sorting through the refuse for food and bottles and cans to sell to vendors who come to collect recyclables. Around the garbage mounds are makeshift homes, constructed of cardboard scraps and plastic. Behind them are corrugated metal shacks, government housing for those in the area.

Our group returns to the car. In the backseat, tears trickle down my cheeks. I begin to sob and ask my youth pastor, Pastor Rick, "Why are we here? What was the point of doing a puppet show for those kids? What difference does it make?"

"Maria, we had a chance to show these kids that God loves them so much that he sent someone to tell them that. We are here to show them that God cares."

"Is that enough?"

I can't stop crying—though I'm not sure whether it's for me or for them. What more can I do, realizing acutely my privilege as a North American? On a global scale, having and not having is all relative. My complaints about hand-me-down clothes have suddenly become petty. While this can easily move into guilt and a patronizing need to help others, the experience wakes me up to see the world in a different light. It changes how I experience and understand God's care.

* * *

I cannot unsee what I saw. That year began a transformation in me in which I went from being enthusiastic about sharing the gospel and serving in different cultural contexts to having mixed feelings about the impact of short-term missions without responsible long-term engagement, questioning trips designed more for those who go than for those who receive us. At the same time, I began to experience God's hand in the world as much bigger and more complex than I had realized. I have been humbled time and again by the faith of those I encountered in places where life is not as materially rich but hospitality and deep spirituality are abundant; I have learned how important mutuality can be.

I needed to learn and receive. *I* had to listen, wait, and see what might be possible only *after* spending time with others.

I sensed a call to open my heart to this reality, to find a way to build bridges and bring resources and people together as a response to relationships and recognition of gifts already present. Even now, these images remind me how important it is for theological formation at a young age to be taken seriously. I will continue to work out over my lifetime how to live with care, compassion, and integrity, stirred by humility and a responsibility for stewarding resources and gifts.

Almost three decades later, my colleague Mark and I traveled with our respective sons (Daniel was fourteen and Joshua was thirteen) to Medellín (Colombia), Guatemala City, and Mexico City in preparation for future pilgrimages. I took them to the very place in Guatemala City I had visited as a teenager. The mounds that I saw decades earlier had an informal settlement built upon them, with walls, and the new garbage dump was several miles away. We were greeted by the leader of the settlement and allowed to walk through it to get a sense of how the community had been constructed, learning about its complicated relationship with the government and the community's unplanned growth and infrastructure.

That day we also went to a garbage dump near El Mercado Central, the city's central market. While there, we learned about a mobile library program for the nearby residents. I chatted with our local host using simple Spanish. We connected as mothers trying to figure out how to raise our children. In the area where people were searching for recyclables and valuables, we saw an elderly woman shouting with excitement. She had found a piece of fish, which she carefully put away for her lunch. She even approached us to show it to us.

I have wondered what my son has kept in his heart from that trip. I didn't realize until I read one of his college application essays how much that experience had impressed him. He recalled the incident with the woman and the fish and connected it with his summer job at a food pantry and seeing neighbors on our floor with the same bags of food he was delivering around the neighborhood. Memory can be a powerful thing. Sharing this moment with him is something that shapes how we see the world and each other as mother and son, and the way God is forming us as a family.

God not only stirred compassion and calling in me on that trip to Guatemala. As I described earlier, the nondenominational Chinese church from which I was sent was relatively conservative. Nothing prepared me for the tangible, embodied experience of spiritual warfare I encountered there.

* * *

I don't know what is wrong with me. It's like there is a weight on my chest. I can't stop crying. We are on our way to share our testimonies at a church in a different part of the city. Along the way, I find myself sobbing, unable to stop.

"Are you okay?"

"I just feel so heavy. There's something pressing on me, on my chest. It feels hard to breathe. I don't know what it is."

"Let's pray."

We finally arrive at the church, and I stumble out of the car. The moment I step across the threshold of the church, I feel as if a brick has been lifted off my chest. I am free. And I am startled. It is like nothing I have ever experienced before.

Yes—I had a supernatural encounter with Christ when I came to believe in him in my late childhood.

Yes—I understand that there is a spiritual world of darkness and God's light.

But this is the most concrete experience of that warfare I have ever had.

I walk up to the front of the church sanctuary with a different understanding of the good news. It is good and real indeed.

"Buenas noches. Me llamo María. Lo siento. Mi español no es muy bueno pero yo quiero compartir el cuento de mi vida con Jesucristo. Gracias por la oportunidad. . . ."

That night, I share my testimony as best as I can in my high-school Spanish. It is the beginning of many cross-cultural encounters that my body remembers as much as my mind does.

* * *

This was a new and very real encounter with the world of spirits, and it shaped what I knew about the power and movement of the Holy Spirit, and how I knew it. It was in the context of an expanded family—a spiritual one that included those with whom I came and those who welcomed me into their church that night—that I began to broaden my experience of who God is and what the good news means. The small group from my church with whom I traveled—my OCM family—was also being changed by the Spirit; some of us—Dong, Sam, Phil, Hang, Melva, and others—went on to serve in pastoral and ministry leadership. If I were not a part of this larger family of God, my experience of worship would have been limited to what I knew from my home and from my Chinatown church.

God's tugging on my heart was now not limited to my exposure to the many testimonies shared in our basement studio at home in Long Island but had expanded to my own firsthand witness of the power of God to quell the darkness. On subsequent short-term mission trips to China, Mozambique (with my sister), and Peru, I began to understand more about what and where God was calling me. I recognized that his power and the path that my life was to take were moving me into cross-cultural spaces for which my third-culture upbringing had prepared me.

My experience of how God moved in the world was expanding and deepening. This was a story shared with a growing family, being formed theologically in conversation and action with a bigger body of Christ than I ever thought possible.

PAUSE AND REFLECT

- Have you ever served on a short-term mission trip? Where did you go? With whom did you go? What happened? What did you learn about God, yourself, and others?

- What does long-term, lifelong mission look like? How is it similar to or different from a short-term trip?
- Do you have time to remember?

* * *

Dear Professor Gornik,

My husband, Tony, and I would like to enroll in the biblical interpretation class. Would it be possible for us to bring our newborn son, Joshua, to class? He is two months old and I'm still nursing him. I'll take him out if he gets distracting.

Thanks for considering our request.

Regards,
Maria and Tony Wong

This is the email we send to Mark (my soon-to-be professor and eventual colleague) a few weeks before our first seminary class. Even as we prepare to become new parents and await the arrival of our oldest son, Joshua, we hear from our Bible study leader at church, Hansen, that it is possible to attend seminary part time without moving out of the city. He and another friend, Eric, from OCM, are enrolled in a master of arts program in urban mission, offered by Pennsylvania-based Westminster Theological Seminary but run by Rev. Mark Gornik in New York.

We have no intention of becoming ordained pastors or full-time mission workers, but we are looking for a way to deepen our theological understanding of how our faith affects life in its entirety. I want to explore how living out the gospel shapes who I am vocationally as an educator, mother, and wife, and Tony wants to explore who he is as a social worker, father, and husband. We have had experiences serving as Bible study and fellowship leaders in our local churches. We have taken a Perspectives in World Missions course together, and have had a taste of what it means to go deeper into theological study. For both of us, it is our second graduate degree, and we do not want to relocate our lives and family for study, especially not with a newborn.

Not knowing where this will lead, Mark responds with a yes.

The rest is history.

* * *

This formal theological education was only possible with extended family supporting our part-time studies as babysitters, conversation partners, and prayer warriors. Tony worked full time in youth development at Children's Aid, and I was piecing together part-time teaching jobs as I stayed home with our infant son. My sister, my parents, my in-laws, and even my great-aunt and her family in Philadelphia were part of our seminary journey, each taking their turn to watch over Joshua while Tony and I were in class. We managed to graduate in three rather than four years, alongside doing ministry, working, and raising our family. And we did so with renewed vision and a deepened calling to stay where we were in the city.

In 2006, the year before we graduated, Mark invited me to join him part time at City Seminary. Instead of juggling three part-time jobs while trying to homeschool Joshua before he went to elementary school, I went with the one part-time job and never left. Moving to full-time work before we had our second son, Josiah, I went on to pursue a doctorate in Adult Learning and Leadership at Teachers College, Columbia University. Now, seventeen years after my first seminary class, I am the provost at City Seminary of New York and codirect a national learning network for ministry in the city.

The opportunity Tony and I had to attend formal seminary training as a family shaped how we see the power of being part of a theological learning community in the city, growing alongside others in ministry praxis. Family has become the heart of City Seminary. We are formed together in this Ephesian moment, reflecting the diversity of the body of Christ. We are tied together through friendship and familial bonds that go beyond blood and culture. Couples, siblings, adult children and retired parents, extended family, church members, and colleagues have come through Ministry Fellows, our nondegree certificate program in urban ministry, seeking to be on the "same page" with regard to faith, ministry, and life.

WE LEAD NYC youth seminary welcomes high school youth and youth leaders to form an intergenerational learning community. The Thriving for Ministry initiative is a peer-learning community for *their* pastors and lay ministry leaders, designed to support flourishing in and for ministry in the city through small groups and retreats. Bible for Life courses provide an overview of Scripture and explore topical application to ministry and life, and our part-time master of arts degree program in "Ministry in the Global City" extends our continuum of lifelong theological formation. Our annual Symposium on Women in Leadership and Ministry (WILAM) makes space to encourage and renew sisters, daughters, aunts, mothers, and grandmothers. Families take part in some or all of these opportunities, at the same time or years apart.

Families also come in and out of the Walls-Ortiz Gallery, previously in our physical gallery space and now online in virtual programs, at the Fresh Oils Community Garden, and at our sidewalk hangout on Tuesday afternoons by the St. Luke Triangle building. Theology as a verb happens as our staff and visitors eat meals together and engage in conversations, art looking, art making, gardening, and much more. These third spaces make possible an active presence of public faith as an institutional good neighbor in the community. Through these activities, families have deepened and expanded our community of ministry learning and practice across generations, cultures, and traditions. They have enabled us to listen better and grow in mutuality and community as we bridge differences across a variety of dimensions.

Our students come from a diversity of ecclesial backgrounds, ranging in affiliation from Pentecostal to Presbyterian. They live throughout the boroughs of New York City, with roots in countries around the world. They are multivocational pastors, church leaders, youth workers, missionaries, and faithful Christians in various occupations. They desire to participate in a larger community of ministry and leadership, to gain tools for fruitful and effective practice, and to have a reflective space to explore vocation and calling. Enriched by their experiences in our learning communities, these families influence church life and leadership in diverse neighborhoods across the city.

Miriam is an associate pastor at a Latino Pentecostal church on the Lower East Side, part of the Council of Damascus Churches, an international network of more than two hundred Latino churches. She is a Ministry Fellow graduate and a leader at the seminary, and she also serves as an officer at the Council level. Miriam is married to Peter, her copastor at the church, who is the principal of their local Bible institute. Until recently, he also worked as a full-time social worker at a Bronx hospital. Now he is focused on building up a private counseling practice. Peter graduated from City Seminary's MA program "Ministry in the Global City" in 2020. Both Nuyoricans, they lead a creative ministry for young adults from their community called Plus One. Miriam's older daughter and Peter's sister, brother-in-law, and mother have all been a part of the Ministry Fellows program. City Seminary is "home" for their family.

Born and raised in Harlem, Adrienne is a community chaplain who also serves at the seminary. She is pastor of a local congregation and healing ministry in Harlem. Her mother, Mother Croskey, a retiree from the New York City public school system, is one of our Ministry Fellows program graduates who regularly volunteers at our annual women's symposium and gallery events. We worked on a children's literacy and planting project with one of Adrienne's daughters, and her three grandsons are regulars at the gallery, community events, and prayer walks around the city. Uncle Jerome and Aunt Barbara recently joined us for an art-making workshop at the Fresh Oils Community Garden.

Oluremi and Toyin are Ministry Fellows graduates from different cohorts. As a couple, they study together in our MA program. While both are leaders at Christ Apostolic Church in East New York, Brooklyn, Toyin is also active in African immigrant advocacy as well as youth ministry. She joined our WE LEAD NYC faculty team a few years ago, and their two daughters, Esther and Debbie, became core members of our youth seminary community, both returning as peer mentors. Her younger daughter Pupo is in middle school and can't wait to be old enough to join.

The list goes on. *Theological education is formation for, with, and by the family, inside and outside of the home.*

* * *

I walk up to the whiteboard and write across the center: "What is family?"

It is spring 2019, and Pastor Vivian and I are teaching the first class of "Family, Youth, and Friendship" with our inaugural cohort of master of arts degree students in the "Ministry in the Global City" program.

Silently, one by one, the students pick up a dry-erase marker and write down a phrase or a word they associate with the prompt. They sit down, see what others have written, and if inspired, return to the board to write some more. After about ten minutes have passed, the students begin the next phase of the silent conversation—making connections with arrows and lines.

We begin to unpack the categories of what has emerged. "Family" turns out to be quite a complicated term, one that comes with both positive and negative associations and emotions. This comes to light in pronounced and eye-opening ways in the case studies students write later in the term. Whether from personal or pastoral and ministry experience, "family" can be a loaded term.

"What is the ideal family in the Bible? Is it one man and one woman, as in Adam and Eve? Is there an ideal?"

"What about Paul and single people? I don't understand the church rhetoric that you are not complete if you are not married or don't have children. Where does that leave those who are not married? So many churches are full of educated, older single women in New York City."

"What about families that are not blood-related? Who really is 'family'?"

* * *

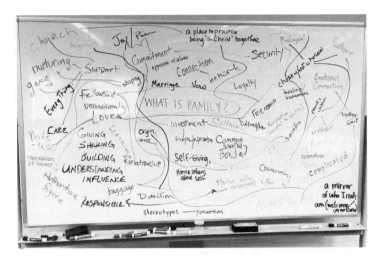

"What Is Family?" chalk talk exercise from MA course "Family, Youth, and Friendship"; photo by author (2019)

* * *

In our first offering of the MA course "Family, Youth, and Friendship," Pastor Vivian and I shared case studies of family ministry experiences, asked students to write about their own experiences, invited guest speakers, and engaged with the complexity of "family" as a concept and reality both in the Bible, historically, and in contemporary times. On one panel, Pastor Vivian reflected on his father, who was a minister and leader in the church, and the legacy of his family. There were pain, suffering, and anguish associated with family. There were draining relationships and lifegiving ones. Sister Marylin and Pastor Huibing shared from their perspectives as single women and elders in the church family. Dr. Tremper Longman examined the place of family and wisdom in the book of Proverbs, while Dr. Ruth Padilla DeBorst described a blended and extended "family" at Casa Adobe, an intentional intergenerational theological community in Costa Rica.

Indeed, home can be both a formative and a nurturing place, a place of formation as well as malformation when it is difficult and fraught with anxiety. It can be a place that may feel suffocating rather than comforting. It can be the site of difficult conversations, silence, or violence, highlighted particularly in recent years across differences in political and generational perspectives. No home is the perfect place and there is no perfect family. And in these pandemic times, what was once a small interpersonal annoyance has the potential to become much more in the everyday. However, this is when "family" of the extended and spiritual kind plays an even more critical role of support and space.

"Family" is not just blood relationships and spiritual community; family in the context of theological formation extends into deep relationships. This can be as cousins, aunts, uncles, grandparents, and stepfamily as well as friends who become "family" for one reason or another. This was the case in the early church, as brothers and sisters came together across cultural, socioeconomic, and gender lines, and this is the case for the contemporary church too. Family is the people that God chooses for us, not necessarily those we choose for ourselves. And attending to family for theological formation is ever more important in light of this reality. Jeremiah 29:4–7 exhorts us to seek the flourishing of the place (and the people) that God has put us in and with, in the families and communities in whose midst we are called to be. As we bear fruit and multiply, the many iterations of these families can grow.

PAUSE AND REFLECT

- How do you define "family" or understand it in your context? What are the ministry implications of that for you, and for your church?
- Consider doing a similar whiteboard exercise in your classroom or with a group of friends. Start in silence and write with pen and paper. In a virtual environment, use Zoom

with a digital whiteboard like Google Jamboard or Padlet for brainstorming and making connections.

- What emerges when you share your thoughts in this way? What patterns and questions do you see that you didn't see before?

* * *

A core theme of our research and our curriculum at City Seminary is generations. Theological formation can happen in the transmission and exchange of faith from one generation to the next, sometimes from the first to the second or third generation, and sometimes the other way around when children bring their parents to church. We are only beginning to appreciate what we can learn from a diversity of church models and traditions.

Rather than limiting theological education as a professional pipeline for ordination of individual clergy, we at City Seminary understand theological formation more broadly, encompassing what Latino theologian Justo González[3] described as a "drip line" that reaches multiple points of impact, from the community to the church and the denomination or ministry governance. Recognizing the range of opportunities in which theological formation can take shape, our model engages with family and community from the start, providing entry points for engagement as early as high school and on through retirement. Learning is lifelong, and it is for the whole church, the priesthood of *all* believers.

Even as we engage pastors and ministry leaders in peer-learning communities, we don't forget that support includes spouses, children, and other forms of family. *The unit of theological education we seek to serve is not simply the one but the many.* But this also means that we have to understand better what this means for the next generation of faith in the city. And this brings us back to learning from the church.

Research and curriculum design go hand in hand. Listening to the next generation and seeing how the church is manifesting itself in a multiplicity of ways in the city mean that we need to be present to who and what is in front of us, and be attentive to how we are responding. WE LEAD NYC began by gathering ministry leaders who love youth and young adults. We shared stories about our own encounters with God and young people, and listened to youth, parents, youth leaders, and pastors through surveys, focus groups, and interviews. Then we spent three years of discovery and exploration of intergenerational theological formation with high schoolers and youth leaders.

The pandemic brought us to a pause. We stopped and listened to our community amid this tidal wave of change. We began again by responding to the needs and questions of young people. Mental health concerns are more critical than ever, and spiritual formation attends to the whole person. The future of the church is in the next generation; theological education and leadership development are meant for them now, not just for and in the future.

This vision for theological formation moves from focusing on the individual to the family and to generations. It is a vision that was cultivated in my home as an MK with my sister; it expanded in Guatemala alongside my church family; it continues to mature with my husband and children; and it is being cultivated with my extended family at City Seminary.

In essence, *City Seminary was built on the coming together of stories, of individuals' and families' lives, for the purpose of becoming God's peace in the city.* While we are a formal institution, the informal theological formation of our children and engagement with our parents interact with the intercultural reality of the work at the seminary. It is in tension with an overwhelming Western societal emphasis on the individual, authenticity, and how meaning is made at the individual level. Our relationships with God and others shape the lives we live—in the open as well as in the intimacy of our homes.

* * *

"Let's start."

Tony and I are now with the two not-so-little ones, Josiah and Immy, in the living room of our apartment. The room has been set up with the couch and chairs facing the piano and music stand. Immy (now seven years old) has graduated to the role of "assistant pastor." She reads Scripture from the front and shares a "word" from God.

This time, Joshua (now fourteen years old) is away at a youth group. I thought that previously he had organized everything for such home church sessions, but I was wrong. Josiah plays songs on a tablet on the dining table, and we sing karaoke style, following the lyrics on YouTube.

A short talk follows worship.

"Today we are going to talk about anger."

Wait: Is this the topic they discussed with Po-Po (婆婆) last week? Or are our kids telling us something indirectly about something they've been noticing? As it turns out, they chose the topic from their devotion book on their own, not prompted by a prior discussion. Should I be relieved?

Josiah wraps up the reading with a closing prayer.

"Coffee hour will now take place at the dining table."

Don't worry: they don't drink coffee (yet). That's just what fellowship time is called at home.

Whether it is something they picked up from us hosting fellowship groups in our apartment twice a week, weekly devotions with Po-Po (婆婆) over Skype, or Sunday service at church, "home church" has now become a part of our family life.

We are parents led by our children in worship.

At home. In community. As a family.

Me, my kitten Mamo, and Meron, a neighbor's child; Gambella Health Science and Teaching College, Ethiopia; photo by a friend (2001)

3

Friends

Do you have time to see?

"Shall we have a coffee ceremony? It's too hot to do anything else."
It is March 2002, and the dry season in Gambella, Ethiopia. That day it is get-
ting close to what feels like 50 degrees Celsius (122 degrees Fahrenheit!). How I
miss the wet season, even if it rains most of the time and the high mosquito-bite
count on our legs and arms, despite repellent and long sleeves, means that
we—Jody, Anne, and I, volunteer instructors at the college—regularly visit the
clinic for a blood test to see if we have malaria in our systems.

Our English classes for students training to be secondary-school teachers
at the Gambella Teacher Training and Health Sciences College are sched-
uled for early in the morning around seven o'clock and in the evening around
eight. It is difficult to get any work done in between. It is simply too hot.

I take out a bag of raw coffee beans, the metal roasting plate, the propane
stove, the jebena (ጀበና coffee pot), cups, spoons, a bottle of filtered water,
sugar, and the incense. We begin a two-hour process of roasting the beans
over the stove, grinding them with a mortar and pestle, letting the coffee boil
and bubble up in the jebena (ጀበና), and pouring three rounds of thick, dense
buna (ቡና coffee); the third round conveys a blessing. Traditionally, we add
a spoon of sugar to each of the small cups, then fill up each one and stir. An
intense, sweet, thick jolt awakens us from our afternoon lethargy amid a
haze of pleasant-smelling incense that sets apart time and space.

We have buna (ቡና) and spend the afternoon together at a neighbor's
house. Sometimes it is next door at Misra's; other times it might be at Jody's
or Anne's. Often our young friends and helpers, Mamush and Mahmoude,
are there. And then we have a much-needed siesta *before dinner and a night*

of evening classes in somewhat cooler temperatures. I'm not sure if there is a particular word for daytime rest in Amharic, but it is definitely a way of life. Somehow the buna (ቡና) doesn't stop us from nodding off.

Even though the pastel pink, yellow, and blue prefabricated connected homes (featured in the opening photo) for faculty on campus have been outfitted for air-conditioning units, an unreliable hydroelectric dam in nearby Metu turns them into the equivalent of brick ovens during the day and even more so at night if you can't open your door because of the mozzies. I arrange for a mosquito net to be installed around the back porch in order to sleep outside and survive. Otherwise, I'll be getting malaria for the eighth time from all the mosquitoes breeding in the drainage water collector behind my house.

I am newly engaged to Tony, as of late summer 2001. He surprises me with a marriage proposal two weeks before I am scheduled to depart for Addis Ababa, the capital of Ethiopia. On the morning of September 11, 2001, I am packing my suitcase for my flight later in the day when he calls and tells me to turn on the TV to watch the news about the first airplane crash. I look out the window of my fifth floor Chinatown apartment and see the smoke. Soon after, I see the second tower collapse. It is an eventful day, most certainly not the one I expected.

I leave a week later after saying "Yes!" and plan for a wedding when I return. I begin a year's stint teaching English pedagogy at the college as part of the International Foundation for Education and Self-Help (IFESH) Teachers for Africa exchange program. The program was started in 1981 by an African American Baptist minister, the Reverend Leon Sullivan, to support educational reform efforts, strengthening teacher training and ministries of education. After four years of teaching elementary music in the South Bronx and graduating earlier that May with a master of arts degree in international educational development, I am ready to go abroad.

Here in Gambella, I slow my normally hurried pace. Time deepens the possibilities of relationship and presence. Extended moments of being together imprint a pattern and value of gathering together to spend relaxed, uninterrupted time with others. Just as the sweet-smelling incense burnt during the afternoon coffee ceremony sets apart time and space, so friendship is made possible through the intentionality of making space for each other.

The extreme weather, the constraints on electricity and water, the shift in pace of life, and the buna (ቡና)-making process are in fact part of friendship as theological formation, allowing me to experience and see the world differently. I slow down. I stop to listen. The rooster crows yet again in the middle of the day. I stop to see. The smoke from the incense during buna (ቡና) lingers before dissipating, stretching time.

I don't romanticize this way of life built around a different cultural geography, but I embrace the importance of learning from others, moving and becoming formed in a different cadence and reality. And I take this home to New York City as a way to resist the syncopated busyness of city life.

* * *

In this chapter, I reflect on the importance of *friends as theological educators.* Friendship expands in circles of people who help shape who we become, some of whom we might not otherwise befriend if not for the gospel bringing unlikely people together. Berber theologian Saint Augustine wrote: "In this world two things are essential: life and friendship."[1] It may be easy to become friends with people who have similar interests, but being a part of the body of Christ assumes only the sharing of a common faith.

Therefore, these friends may be used by God to change and stretch as well as sustain us. We cross cultural barriers, socioeconomic strata, and power dynamics, and form unexpected bonds, with people with very different backgrounds and experiences. Friendships such as these can shake as much as shape, and reveal to us more of ourselves than we might care to admit; yet in the midst of it all, we may be transformed together into a more clear, colorful, and plural image of God.

British writer C. S. Lewis most poignantly describes friendship in the plural as he reflects on the death of his mutual friend Charles Williams and his ongoing friendship with J. R. R. Tolkien: "In each of my friends there is something that only some other friend can fully bring out. By myself I am not large enough to call the whole man into activity; I want other lights than my own to show all his facets. Now that Charles is dead, I shall never again see Ronald's [Tolkien's] reaction to a specifically Charles joke. Far from having more of Ronald, having him 'to myself' now that Charles is away, I have less of Ronald."[2]

Lewis goes on to describe friendship as resembling heaven, with the multitude of the "blessed" increasing what we have of God; the seraphim in Isaiah 6:3 cry, "Holy, holy, holy," as we all share the "Heavenly Bread" among us. The more we share, the more we have together. And yet, paradoxically, the less we share in common, the more potential there is to know ourselves and others better because of difference.

I have explored this paradox of diversity in my research and have found that a difference in perspectives adds to and enriches our understanding of the world, and indeed, our ability to theologize with wisdom. It helps us distinguish our cultural lenses from those of others. As such, diversity in friendships and in learning cohorts forms the basis of relational knowledge as theological formation at City Seminary of New York. If you want to learn about Pentecostalism, is it better to read a book about it or befriend someone who is Pentecostal? Perhaps even better, do both, *and* go worship with them at their church.

The stories I share here trace my journey back to this life-changing season in Ethiopia with lifelong friends I never expected to see multiple times after I left, further back into my childhood and three high school prayer partners, and the circle of friends who challenged how I lived out and shared my faith during a year abroad studying in London. From these reflections, I turn to the ways friends as theological educators have helped me to see friendship as a learning outcome at the seminary. From seminary colleagues to a cohort model of learning in community, theological formation comes by being deeply informed and shaped by relationships that go beyond blood ties. These are at the heart of the church and of whatever hope we have for a theological education that manifests itself inside the classroom and beyond, in the interstitial spaces of meals eaten in homes and on picnic blankets, and of subway rides taken together.

* * *

"Is this your first time in Africa?"
"Yes."

It is my first domestic flight from Addis Ababa to Gambella, a town 40
kilometers from the Sudanese border. The Ethiopian habesha (ሐበሻ) man
sitting next to me is curious about this young Chinese woman speaking En-
glish with an American accent on a plane headed west.
"Where are you going? Will you get off at Jimma?"
Jimma is the stop in between Addis and Gambella.
"No, I am going to Gambella to teach there."
"What? Gambella? It is so hot there. And the people are black!"

* * *

This was my introduction to colorism in Ethiopia. Many of the
habesha (ሐበሻ) tribes—Amharic, Oromo, Tigrinya, etc.—are
lighter brown in skin tone and have wavy black hair with texture
reminiscent of Indians from South Asia. Gambella was close to
Sudan, so the nomadic Anuak and Nuer tribes lived in villages
in the area. They are tall, slender, and darker in skin tone. From
teaching in the South Bronx in New York City, I was headed to
what might be seen as the South Bronx of Ethiopia.

I know what it feels like to be seen and treated differently because of my appearance. This is not only in the context of being
a minoritized individual in America, but also in the way I move
about the world in cross-cultural settings like this one. I am ambivalent about being labeled a "person of color" (POC); I don't
really position my identity in reference to whiteness. I am neither
white nor black, but am I yellow? Maybe caramel.

I also know what it feels like to be seen as a little "less" within
my own cultural community. A lighter, whiter complexion is seen
as beautiful in Chinese culture; the evidence is in all those Asian
whitening and skin-lightening cosmetics. I have chosen not to respond to comments from family members and others in my community about how easily I turn and stay brown in the summer into
winter. Colorism is everywhere, even if racism is a more dominant
concept in the United States than elsewhere in the world.

While my plane-seat neighbor was well meaning and kind
(he worked at a local nongovernmental organization [NGO] and
showed up at my home on campus two days later with two white kit-

tens whom I named Mamo and Mamush, one of which is pictured in the opening image of this chapter), this was a lesson in recognizing cultural realities that I had not anticipated but that resonated for me. Of course, at the same time, most of the people I encountered in Ethiopia also did not expect *me* to come to teach English pedagogy; little children and strangers that I passed by in the village called out "China-China" or ferenji (ፈረንጅ foreigner). Again, my accent—now American—confused those I encountered.

There was a community of ferenjis (ፈረንጅ) already there when I arrived. There were Idris and Veronica, two Nigerian government volunteer nurses teaching in the health sciences department. Two volunteer faculty from Voluntary Service Overseas (VSO) were there—Jody, half English and half Swedish, taught English, and Anne from Wales taught in the science department. Two other VSO volunteers from England taught in the local high school.

Father Richard, a Maryknoll missionary from New York, had been working with Sudanese refugees in the area for several years and left for the United States shortly after I arrived. Father Angelo and other Catholic priests from Rome had built campuses equipped with a parish house, a church, and an open area surrounded by walls topped with barbed wire and patrolled by a security guard. They were interested in youth programs and set up multipurpose facilities.

The Catholic doctors from Milan who came later went to the clinic in Abobo, a few hours away, and the Sisters of Charity from India and the Philippines ran the orphanage in town. A group of Catholic Yarumal apostolic missionaries from Latin America; three priests from Colombia, Fathers Niko, Arturo, and Joseph; and a lay brother from Costa Rica arrived around the time I did from an assignment in Kenya; they went farther out to the villages of Lare and Pugnudo, more than three hours away, to learn the local languages of the Anuak and Nuer.

I never imagined I would later reconnect with Fathers Niko and Arturo, in their home country, Colombia. I also befriended one of their colleagues, Father Tulio, who was in the Bronx at a Yarumal mission home and left for Ethiopia after I returned to New York. He returned to New York years later to pastor in a parish in the Bronx and become part of the City Seminary of New York learning community. He came to speak to our MA students shortly before I took the group to Medellín, Colombia, on an urban pilgrimage. There, the students met Fathers Niko and Arturo. Life comes full circle. Again.

Our long talks and walks, and opportunities to test out my manual driving skills in their pickup trucks on the bumpy rural roads, led to my inquiries about their missional approach, which contrasted with those of the other Catholic and, less visible to me, Pente (ኣንጤ Protestant) missionaries. They began with listening and learning first: "Live with people. See them for who they are. Learn their language. Attune yourself to the culture, and see where God invites you in." This resonated very much with me.

The Yarumal Society for Foreign Missions from Colombia was the first Latin American Catholic apostolic order, established in 1927, to be sent out specifically for primary evangelization to those unreached by the gospel and with a preference for the most poor. Members of this order often worked in remote areas and sought to help people to "find beauty in belonging to a Christian family," living with the love of Christ. They focused on the "simplicity of life, meeting basic needs, and responding to social and development needs," carefully and in collaboration with the community.[3] Because they came from a country with a history of civil unrest, they understood the experience of violence and the fragility of peace. They knew what it meant to be located on the border of Sudan, with a soldiers' post near the college. I looked forward to regular deep spiritual conversations with them whenever they came to Gambella, or when I could visit them during the weekends or breaks.

Truth be told, I chose to go to Ethiopia as a volunteer teacher, not as a missionary. I had mixed feelings about the historical implications tied to colonization; the imposition of power, values, and culture; and—from my graduate studies in international educational development—the problematic and unsustainable technical-assistance NGO model. I wanted to be on campus without a Christian mission agenda or affiliation. I had something to offer as an educator and native English speaker to my students, who were tasked with becoming English teachers upon graduation, but I knew I would learn much more from my students, my colleagues, and the community there about living life with different eyes and experiences of time and relationship.

My faith followed me to Ethiopia. There was no separation of sacred and secular. Whether I was teaching, having a coffee ceremony with friends, or hosting a women's club for female students, I found myself being formed theologically and missiologically in a milieu of interreligious life.

I broke fast during Ramadan with my other next-door neighbor Misra (the wife of my colleague Solomon). She became a good friend and taught me to make buna (ቡና) and injera (አንጀራ) properly, even though she knew very little English and my Amharic was limited at best. She made the most delicious samosas. Sometimes verbal language is not necessary.

I had intense theological debates with Bisau (Solomon's brother), who was Muslim, and with Tewodros, a passionate Pente (ጴንጤ) student who had been thrown out of his house because his Christian faith was different from his family's Ethiopian Orthodox tradition.

And then there was Jody, who was suspicious of organized faith. She, in particular, challenged me to reflect on transparency and consistency of faith in action. Her critical questions and observations were persistent, sometimes jaded. I learned as much from her skepticism as I did from the faithful resilience I witnessed in others. Friendship with her was not always easy—she was very much an extrovert, and I an introvert. But she helped me to grow to see the world with her eyes.

I celebrated Catholic Mass for a year in a trilingual church—worshiping in Amharic, Nuer, and Anuak; while I couldn't follow everything, at least the rhythms of the liturgy and Scripture were familiar. I read along in English. And I was grateful for Anne, whose Protestant faith was closer to my own. She had already set the stage with her connections with the priests for those occasional stops to the parish house after service, for cheese and chocolate treats imported from Italy! They were from Rome, after all.

A local friend with whom I still keep in touch is Mamush, my house helper. At the time, he was a secondary-school student nine years my junior. As was the agreement with other ferenji (ፈረንጅ) volunteers and local secondary-school students, I paid him monthly to bring me the oh-so-brown water from the nearby Baro River for flushing the Western toilet installed in my home that had plumbing but no running water, and for bucket bathing. The water had to be boiled and filtered for drinking and cooking.

He rode the red bike to the market to get food when I was busy, and became very concerned when, during the first week of classes, I came down with the first (and worst) of my seven cases of malaria that year. I was sick for a full week, and he cooked dinner every day for me to make sure I survived. Over time, I came to trust him with just about everything.

Mamush even told me one day about a student who was trying to bribe him to steal the answers for a makeup exam from my home. We concocted a plan to give the student another version of the exam in order for Mamush not to get in trouble for telling me the truth. The expression on the student's face when he realized that the actual makeup questions were different from the ones for which he had prepared was priceless.

When we had time at the end of a long day, Mamush and I would sit on the porch and talk about life. Mamush is Ethiopian Orthodox. I asked him about his faith, his family, and his dreams. He was the little brother I never had. It was hard to leave Gambella, and Mamush in particular, when I boarded the flight to Addis Ababa to head home. I thought it was the last time I'd ever see him.

I have had the opportunity to see him twice since then, when I returned to Ethiopia for work and again when I took students on pilgrimage to Addis Ababa, where he showed them around. While I initially helped to support his undergraduate studies, he went on to get a government scholarship for graduate school. Now he is a professor, doctoral candidate, and research director at Gambella University and has a beautiful wife! Granted, in our friendship there was a power dynamic that involved me coming to his home context as a ferenji (ፈረንጅ) and employer;

however, somehow there came the possibility for friendship that transcended the geographies of where we called "home" and our positionality. We remain connected via Facebook, as I do with former students and friends from Ethiopia, and I hope to see him once again when travel is easier after the pandemic.

There are many complicated dynamics at work in this story of friends, the reasons why the missionary groups were there and how they approached mission work, how I came to be present with this group, and what it meant for me, a North American Chinese woman, to be in the midst of it all. At a time where the colonial implications of missions are under critique more than ever, it was significant that I was who I was. I was neither white nor black. I was a British-born Asian North American, minoritized in one context while seen as foreign in another (or both), representing a story of hybridity that made my relationships with these locals and other ferenji (ፈረንጅ) all the more important.

Crossing these cultural boundaries was critical to the informal theological formation that happened through our conversations and interactions. Worshiping in multiple languages, in different traditions, with those I did not always understand and who did not always understand me helped me to interrogate my own cultural understandings and practices. As I observed what faith meant in life for each of these friends, I experienced bodily the importance of relationships, of living life together in the messiness of miscommunication and forgiveness.

Seeing, hearing, drinking buna (ቡና), eating, and living life together helped to expand our understanding of how big God is, and a microcosm of the Ephesian moment was present again in this small border town in Ethiopia. It prepared me to appreciate the paradox of diversity and to bear witness to how God moved in us, shaping us in his image even as we looked and sounded so different. I would never have imagined that these friends stretched my theological imagination and reality and prepared me for the joy-work I am doing now, again in community with friends, at City Seminary in New York City.

Pause and Reflect

- Put this book down, put the kettle on, and invite someone over for conversation and tea, or maybe three rounds of buna (ቡና). What happens when you stop to listen? How are you present with this person and others? How are they present with you?
- Who do you see and hear around you—those who are familiar or perhaps not—who might change your life if you open yourself up to their friendship? Look through your contacts and social media. Who are your friends? Who might you invite into a relationship that you have not yet dared to?

* * *

"Let's meet at the third-floor prayer room before Cana."

It is my senior year in high school, and I am one of the Cana High School youth group peer leaders at Oversea Chinese Mission (OCM). I have come back from the summer mission trip to Guatemala I described earlier, sobered, inspired, and challenged to live my faith with integrity and purpose.

Oli, who is a sophomore, gives her life to Christ at an OCM winter conference we attend together that year. Thi, a junior, has grown up attending a smaller Vietnamese church in the Lower East Side and, later, Brooklyn with her family. She decides to attend OCM on her own during high school. Mi had gone to OCM with her family early on as a child but stopped going for a while. She just started attending our youth group the fall before that conference, after a stint attending the Chinese-speaking fellowship group. That memorable winter conference is the catalyst, and the four of us commit to a practice of regular prayer together. We become the TOMM girls, putting the first initials of our names together.

Our lifelong friendship solidifies in that prayer room. We huddle together on the padded bench against white walls that frame the room. The door we close isn't entirely soundproof, and even as we pray aloud, we can hear people passing by talking and laughing in the hallway outside.

We pour out our worries about family, school, and just about everything. Thi remembers it as the first time she is with a peer-led group, not told by an authority figure what to do. Oli, new in the faith, is learning how to pray. We figure out how to do this as we go along, and give it all to God. And we are changed in the process.

A photo of us taken that year for the Cana Caper youth group newsletter resurfaces somewhere on Facebook.

Someone posts a comment: "You guys look the same!"

I think we still do, give or take a few gray hairs.

* * *

It has been almost three decades of friendship and life together. Mi, Thi, Oli, and I are a year apart; Mi and I graduated in the same school year. Oli is the youngest and Mi the oldest. We serve in different churches in the metropolitan New York area, raising our families with young children. We typically meet a few times a year (usually during the Christmas break, Chinese New Year, and for birthdays), though we are much more connected over WhatsApp for prayer requests and updates.

A few years ago, we spent a season reflecting on our spiritual formation together. We explored what kept us together as friends for all this time. We wondered why we had stayed in the city, growing in service and leadership at our respective churches over time. Over six months, we met monthly in our homes and in restaurants around the city to talk about topics ranging from our immigrant families' faith practices and traditions and our husbands' faith backgrounds to parenting our young children in the city. We tried to keep up with our conversations through journals, documenting along the way.

As we began to unpack our stories, we realized that even though we had been friends for such a long time, there had been gaps in connecting amid college, jobs, babies, and busy lives. Taking time to share our faith stories became significant because it revealed even more how that overlap in our lives in high school was formative to each of us. At the start, we confessed thinking that we probably had pretty boring testimonies, remembering that we were "good girls" when we were young. We learned there was much more to each of us than we knew.

Even though we are all Chinese American women, our backgrounds are different. Mi's family is from Wenzhou, China. She recalls that, during her childhood, her Christian parents hosted prayer meetings at home in China. In fact, her grandparents became Christians through Western missionaries, tracing a connection to Hudson Taylor. Oli's family and mine are from Hong Kong, but they emigrated to different countries at different stages of life. Her parents went to university in the United States, while my parents were educated in the United Kingdom and Hong Kong. My sister and I grew up in a Christian home, whereas she and her brother did not. It was her grandmother who prayed fervently for her family to come to faith. A family friend brought Oli to youth group during high school. Thi's family is originally from Vietnam, and she straddled attending her parents' smaller evangelical Vietnamese church (which they founded as the first of its kind in the tristate area) and our larger nondenominational Chinese church. Our lives intersected in high school at our church youth group.

We interviewed our husbands to find out more about their families' faith experiences. We discovered that none of our husbands had grown up in Christian homes. Without parenting models to reference, we all had to work out family traditions on our own.

Many of our conversations have been about how to parent as second-generation Chinese American Christians. Our children range from eight to eighteen years of age, and we have one to three children each. Two of us live in Manhattan, one lives in Brooklyn, and one recently moved to Long Island. Two of us grew up in the suburbs, and two of us grew up in the city. We are professionals: a doctor, an architect, a higher education administrator, and an educator-scholar.

After all these years, *what* is it that has kept us together and in the faith? It is hard to pinpoint one thing. But there was something in *being formed as young people together*, during a time when prayer was the only thing that made sense as we were wrestling with questions of life and teenage angst, and trying to understand our parents and what to make of ourselves and our future. Somehow, the certainty of God's presence and our prayers in that room on the second floor held us fast to each other *and* to God.

PAUSE AND REFLECT

- Who are your childhood friends? Who keeps you honest and grounds you in your faith?
- Take a moment and draw a circle. Write down the names of the people who are helping you to grow in your questions about everyday life. Add another circle. Write the names of others with whom you would like to go deeper. Do the circles overlap? What other circle of names could you add?

* * *

"Why is that in your notebook?"

"Oh, that's from the church I've been going to on Wednesdays for Bible study."

"Why would you go to church if you had a choice?"

During my junior year in college, I return to the country where I was born and spend a transformative year studying in London, learning some of the hardest lessons of apologetics I will ever learn. A church bulletin I slip into a notebook as a bookmark becomes fodder for intense conversations with friends and dormmates who are Muslims, Hindus, charismatics, agnostics, ethical humanists, and atheists. Apparently, if you are a Christian in the United Kingdom and actually attend church, it is something for which you have to answer.

The year in London challenges me to know and share who I am as God's "beloved." It is the life curriculum that prepares me for the next adventure, and the next. It is the year I learn to take risks—some perhaps less wise than others. And it is the year that I feel as if I finally grow up. I am twenty.

* * *

That year I came to own my faith in a way I never had before. Service and compassion motivated by my Christian faith was not a project but a process, and friendship sprouted in unexpected ways. I walked the streets of London with friends and literally sat down to pray on sidewalks; it was an early version of the "pray and break bread.NYC" community events that have come to be a foundational practice of knowing, loving, and praying for the city in our seminary life. And there was a circle of friends in college and beyond through and with whom I was changed.

I still see Neil every time I have the chance to go to London. He is now a pastor in nearby Croydon. We were in the English department together, and I learned how he wielded his words and passion for Christ in person and on paper. His fire for Christ would wear down almost anyone he encountered, for better or worse. Our friendship encouraged me to be bold and confident in the face of possible rejection.

Oi-may, another friend from the English department, was a British Chinese Christian. We shared a love for Shakespeare, language, and good design. And we were able to talk about what it meant to be a triple minority in majority culture as women, Christians, and Asians living in the UK and USA. Decades later, we remain in touch as she lives in a neighboring state, having married a Chinese American and emigrated to the United States.

And then there was Jane, who lived in the same dorm. "If you really believe, God will give you the gift of tongues." I waited. I believed. And I *still* wait. Jane came from a charismatic background, and we had long talks over tea and crumpets about life and faith. It was good to have someone with whom to process my questions about the experience of tongues and the Holy Spirit, though earnest prayer after prayer was answered with a "no" or a "not yet."

I went to London that year with two friends from Barnard. One of them, Yoon, was a Korean American Christian who studied at the Slade School of Art. On Wednesdays, we went to St. Helen's for "Read-Mark-Learn" Bible study. It was an Anglican church similar in some ways to Redeemer Presbyterian Church, which we attended in New York City. On Sundays, we attended a charismatic church, St. Paul's Onslow Square. We were comfortable moving around during Spirit-filled worship at St. Paul's, sometimes led by our friend Nick, but I was new to hearing people pray in tongues and watching them fall to the floor "slain in the Spirit." It was the time of the Toronto Blessing, and there was tension between churches that were "Bible believing" and others that emphasized more charismatic expressions of worship.

It was theological formation in the unity and diversity of the church, as these churches opened us up to different ways of worshiping God. We experienced both the close reading of Scripture and Spirit-filled music and movement. Yet we did not have to choose one over the other. And while I still don't speak in tongues, I am probably more "Presbycostal" than anything else. Indeed, these friendships with Neil, Oi-May, Jane, and Nick opened up new worlds to us, and gave Yoon and me the space to ask questions and wrestle with unfamiliar aspects of faith and worship.

The list of people and places could go on, but I end here with Paul and Stuart, two men I met during weekly Friday Christian Union campus fellowship distribution of tea, cookies, and sandwiches on the streets. My route was along the Strand, and I learned about the "dole" (a government benefit for the unemployed) and people on the street waiting for government housing. I met up with Paul or Stuart, or sometimes both, on Friday evenings and other days that year. We listened to free opera in the park, and they treated me to tea and apple pie at McDonalds, returning hospitality in a way that dignified our friendship. And when I finally left London to return home, it was Paul and Stuart who saw me off to Heathrow.

There was a power dynamic there as well, a difference in class and privilege. But for me, our friendships were theologically transformative. Befriending them gave me an opportunity to ask questions about life in a way I might never fully understand, to enter into relationship, and to wonder with them how God was at work. They didn't necessarily share my faith, but I came to value the importance of conversations over afternoon tea and spending time together being present and listening. Their friendship was a gift I will not forget.

* * *

The three stories I have shared describe circles of friends that have created space to hold frustration, lament, and joy. Crossing cultural boundaries, generations, and life experiences is an important aspect of theological formation, of making sense of how our Christian faith helps us interpret and understand our questions, as we learn to see and experience the world outside our own bubbles. David Whyte writes this: "Friendship is a mirror to presence and a testament to forgiveness. Friendship not only helps us see ourselves through another's eyes, but can be sustained over the years only with someone who has repeatedly forgiven us for our trespasses as we must find it in ourselves to forgive them in turn. A friend knows our difficulties and shadows and remains in sight, a companion to our vulnerabilities more than our triumphs, when we are under the strange illusion we do not need them."[4]

Whyte goes on to describe that what underlies real friendship is understanding, tolerance, mercy, and "continued, mutual forgiveness." The friends that have held me as I have wept from the pain of being misunderstood, of being accused of intentions other than what I have had in my heart, and of hoping to be forgiven when I have hurt others—these are the friends that sustain me. These are friends that keep me honest, who say the words I don't want to hear but nonetheless need. These are friends with whom I have journeyed and who have not given up on me. And these are also friends I walk with at City Seminary.

* * *

Lord you are so good
Lord you are kind
Lord you are wonderful
My God you are excellent.

Excellent is your name
Excellent is your power
Lord you are wonderful
My God you are excellent.[5]

Pastor Ade, a Nigerian Pentecostal pastor and my seminary colleague, leads us in this now familiar chorus and into prayer with our first cohort of Ministry Fellows, our first nondegree certificate program. It is the fall of 2009, and we are beginning a more than ten-year journey together, building a learning community of New Yorkers who are pastors, ministry and church leaders, and missionaries from across the five boroughs and metropolitan area. They are as young as under twenty-five and as old as over seventy.

We move from administering another seminary's MA degree in urban mission to building and testing our own way of doing urban theological education. We have spent a year reimagining what a graduate degree in ministry in the city could be, and now we have a chance to try out ideas through this nondegree program.

"Let's get the chart paper up and markers out. I'll write up the questions we've been asking, and we can take some time to work out each one."

Mark, our seminary director; Laura, who has earned an MA in urban mission; Pastor Ade; and I work together for months to design the Ministry Fellows curriculum. Over prayer, worship, laughter, meals, back-and-forth conversation when we need to work out differences, many Post-it Notes, markers, and chart paper, we lean into friendship and the gifts of the team. Mark's research on world Christianity, study of the history of New York City, pastoral experience from the Reformed tradition, and experience in community development; Laura's pastoral experience in counseling in a nondenominational church in Queens and contemplative gift of asking good questions; Pastor Ade's Pentecostal church planting and bivocational business background; and my work in facilitating interactive educational spaces, engaging creativity, and building learning communities—all this together opens up possibilities for this approach to theological education for busy New York-

ers. As we listen to and learn from each other, the seeds of our present-day City Learning Ecology programming at the seminary are nurtured to life.

* * *

It is the beginning of many things. And yet it is a continuation of a vision to seek God's peace in the city through theological education, a charism that is beginning to bear more visible fruit as our community expands and deepens.

"I looked around, and there they were. Right in front of me, in this room."

Mark often refers to this, how he came to discover the core of our learning community. They were us. First, students and then staff and faculty. Our grassroots model has literally grown up from the inside out; we are now colleagues and friends.

In every iteration of the Ministry Fellows program, we tell the story of City Seminary. Students read a chapter from Mark's book, *Word Made Global*, about faith moving from one continent to another, alongside an article we have cowritten about the church in New York City. Mark shares how he came to be transformed by his experience with African diaspora churches in New York City, and I speak about how my journey of faith from Asia to the United Kingdom and to New York City came to join his. Sometimes Bishop Vivian joins us, tracing his roots from the island of Jamaica. Other times Pastor Geomon, who is South Indian Pentecostal, or Minister Miriam, who is Nuyorican Pentecostal, joins the group. Whoever shares gives a part of the picture of the Ephesian moment that we are experiencing together.

But becoming community is not a simple process. Setting norms for communication and interaction and unpacking assumptions at the outset of meetings with staff or learning journeys with students are part of how we nurture trust and build relationships. White ethicist Christine Pohl's *Living into Community* is also a key text for us. We recognize the importance that gratitude, promise keeping, truth telling, and hospitality, among other key practices, play for us so we don't take for granted who we are with and what we have together.

While our seminary staff is diverse across cultures and Christian traditions, we gather regularly together for chapel, led by our seminary spiritual director, Sister Marylin, to engage in contemplative prayer and reflect together. Recently, we began the Ignatian spiritual exercises as a staff learning community to walk through together over nine months. Creating shared opportunities as individuals and as a community to be formed deeply in prayer, we provide a common experience and space for interaction. This also happens with our dean of teaching and curriculum Sarah leading us in a variety of learning trips around the city, providing material for life together.

However, with difference comes the potential for misunderstanding. Even with the best of intentions, things can be and have been misperceived or taken in the wrong way. The messiness of intercultural communication requires patience, humility, tears, forgiveness, and reconciliation. There have also been times in which repair and reconciliation may not be as quick in coming as we hope.

Yet we persist, sobered and formed by earlier experiences of working things out with friends, living into the cost and necessity of being willing to stay in difficult conversations. If not in the church, where else can and should this hard work happen? There are still prickly and awkward moments that are necessary for us to work through to illuminate the various ways we see and make meaning of the world. However, this done in friendship and community, remaining with each other, makes possible a future of growth and sustainability.

* * *

"I've been watching the news about what's happening with anti-Asian violence. It seems kind of distant, and I haven't really talked to anyone about it. Last year, with the Black Lives Matter protests, a friend from the seminary called to check in on me. But this year, I'm trying to figure out how to respond. How are you doing?"

I smile. It's the two of us on Zoom, and while we had some other things to discuss, it is an opportunity to catch up on life before talking shop. I am grateful in this moment for Rex, a Ghanaian American colleague, and for our friendship over the years. He has been in my home for meals and meetings, and we've had other heart-to-heart talks about life.

He has also been a bridge for my mother-in-law, who spent most of her life in the Chinatown community and has experienced her own share of racism. Once, while watching my kids at home before I arrived for a dinner meeting, she was hesitant to let Rex in because she didn't know him. But now she recognizes and welcomes him in, understanding who I work with and am friends with in the seminary community, including Black colleagues. It may seem like a simple thing, but it is not.

"Thanks for asking. I really appreciate you reaching out. I actually just had this conversation with the Asian American women in my church small group last night. It's been intense and yet familiar to what we've faced our whole lives."

We spend over an hour talking about the history of Asian American violence and discrimination, Black-Asian dynamics, childhood stories, and our personal identity politics. I see how God is at work in our walking with each other, wrestling theologically with matters of faith and life, able to process in the moment with each other rather than create projects or programs for this purpose.

* * *

As the early church did, at City Seminary we daily take on the work of making small decisions, giving grace, listening first, waiting to speak, and being willing to lament and grieve before healing comes. And the bond we cultivate is not simply over many meals, prayer walks around the city, pilgrimages to other cities, and laughter in homes and on the street. It is through a commitment to walk alongside others serving in the city, for we are becoming signs of God's shalom together with unexpected friends from very different backgrounds and experiences.

With gratitude, we see, hold, and hear each other. In a world where social media algorithms keep us locked in like-minded bubbles, this kind of slow, stumbling, stretching, and at times painful working out of relationships and communication is what forms us theologically as the collective *imago Dei*, in the many hues and shades of the body of Christ as flesh.

* * *

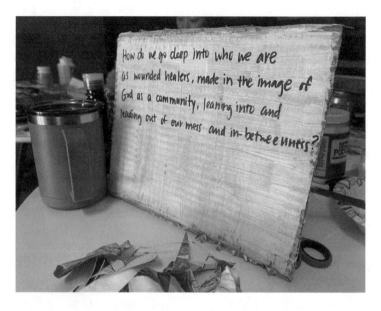

How do we go deep into who we are as wounded healers, made in the image of God as a community, leaning into and leading out of our mess and in-betweenness?

Guiding question for a Thriving in Ministry women's Collaborative Inquiry (CI) group; photo by author (2021)

* * *

"Come on in around the side of the house. We are in the backyard!"

It is another hot summer day, but this time I am in Far Rockaway, Queens. I am in the company of five women pastors and ministry leaders in one of our Thriving in Ministry Collaborative Inquiry groups. The five women don't know each other before the start of the season; I'm the only one they know. With intention, groups are formed from a diversity of backgrounds and Christian traditions. We are white, Black, Asian, and Latina, from Presbyterian, Pentecostal, Anglican, and nondenominational churches. It is the fourth of eight monthly meetings we will have, and our first on-site gathering after starting out online on Zoom. Bev, one of the group members, has invited us to her home.

"How do we go deep into who we are as wounded healers, made in the image of God as a community, leaning into and leading out of our mess and

in-betweenness? As we think about how to answer our question, let's start by visualizing our 'mess.' What does it look like? Use the materials on the table to make something that shows the group what your 'mess' is in your leadership or ministry context."

We lead the sessions by rotation. It is Eunice's turn. She has asked us to bring materials, and we discover our mutual affinity for creative endeavors, evidenced by the abundance of arts and crafts supplies each person has contributed. Beyond the handwritten sign in this photo are piles of scissors, colored and patterned papers, ribbon, yarn, stickers, glitter, ModPodge adhesive, markers, and pens. Some materials are contained in impressive plastic organizers, neatly arranged by category.

The stories that emerge are colorful and textured. The paper, yarn, and ribbon take on lives of their own, as they are shredded, torn, cut apart, tied together, and glued in a variety of arrangements.

While we listen and share, there are moments of silence, tears, and laughter. Then, we move about the space, settling into a comfortable outdoor patio chair or staying in the cool of the air-conditioning of the newly converted garage-become-"man cave." Apparently, the room doubles as the site for the online worship service for Bev's church. We take time to write journal reflections.

Our time that day ends not with buna (ቡና) but with a delicious meal made by Bev and her extended family. Tanya's famous mac 'n' cheese. Ribs. Salad. Bev's signature banana pudding. Our lives become knit together in friendship through conversation, being with each other, prayer, worship, and food; growth and healing become possible. Time and space are necessary for us to see signs of joy and hope, peace and justice, in this between-the-times present and future. At the end of the first season, the group unanimously agrees to continue to meet for another round the following year.

We see each other and bear witness to how God is at work in our lives and throughout the city. This is theological education borne out of friendship for a changing urban world.

Learning with all of our senses on the street; City as Site residency, School of
Visual Arts; photo by Ed Woodham (2017)

4

Learning

Do you have time to listen?

"*Let's go outside.*"

Not sure what to expect, our City as Site residency class follows our instructor, Ed, from the classroom out into the street. We walk out the door, turn north at the corner, and then make a left on West Twenty-Third Street.

We stop in a cluster as we pass a Peloton shop.

"*Go ahead," Ed says. "Lie down on the sidewalk on your backs and close your eyes. Just listen. Pay attention to what you hear for ten minutes. Don't worry. I'll be here.*"

Wondering if he knows what he's talking about, our group tentatively follows his instructions. We spread out along the edge of the hard, gray concrete sidewalk; lie down on our backs; squint and then close our eyes, finding relief from the hot sun. We arrange ourselves head to toe in a row, with a few next to each other, along the edge of West Twenty-Third Street, next to the bike lane seen in this opening image.

A brief moment of silence. Confident footsteps hesitate and pause. Whispers.

"*It's a protest! It's gotta be a protest.*"

There is a murmur of explanation from our protector, Ed.

More footsteps pause and then move on.

Honk! Honk! Beeeeeeep! Honk! Cars move and pause with the traffic. No, that is definitely a truck, a very big truck!

A bicycle whizzes by. A breeze touches my skin. It's too close for comfort.

Another truck slows down. The window rolls down. "Hey! If you want sun, go to the beach! Crazy people."

After an eternity, Ed speaks. "Okay, open your eyes. Without getting up, look up and around you for another ten minutes."

What am I doing here? What did I sign up for?

This exercise, part of a social-practice arts workshop entitled "Beauty + Purpose = Action," led by artist Ed Woodham, is the beginning of work to be done in preparation for a two-hour public intervention to be implemented here on West Twenty-Third Street between Sixth and Seventh Avenues only thirty-six hours later.

We spend another half hour walking the block, looking, listening, smelling, tasting the atmosphere.

What am I doing here? What is "beauty"?

Two days later I am back on the sidewalk. This time I have a blue yoga mat; a plaid green, yellow, and orange knit blanket; a turquoise blue Whole Foods thermal bag holding two large bottles of cold spring water; clear plastic cups; colored sidewalk chalk; and neon plastic containers of soap solution and bubble wands left over from my children's birthday parties.

The introvert in me is petrified.

But I do have a plan. I define "beauty" as the serendipitous encounter between strangers. "Purpose" is the practice of hospitality, and "action" is what I am about to do under the sweltering hot sun in high-80s-degree weather for two hours at midday, midweek, on a busy New York City street.

I lay my yoga mat down on the sidewalk and the picnic blanket on top of it, a few squares of concrete away from the bus stop, the first of four locations I have identified for my four thirty-minute intervals. I make sure I am not too close to the supermarket fruit and vegetable display, and under the shade of a tree. The midday sun is not kind.

I unzip the thermos bag and pull out plastic cups and a bottle of cold water. I fill a cup. I drink. The containers of soap for blowing bubbles come out next and then the sidewalk chalk. I write in bright colors on the sidewalk next to me: "Do you have time to remember?"

I sit down facing the supermarket, and wait. Again, I am waiting.

A white girl with purple hair in her twenties approaches. I offer her a drink of water and a bubble wand, which she accepts with a smile. She settles down beside me. She blows bubbles. I blow bubbles.

"Are you taking classes this summer too?"

Apparently, she is taking a painting studio residency at School of Visual Arts, the same school this residency is a part of. She is exploring some profound ideas, dark and introspective. I sense anxiety and pain in the way she describes the color, texture, and depth of her work.

She takes a piece of red chalk and outlines an image next to the text I have written. She returns to the blanket.

Then a tall, lanky tourist from England stops and takes a look at us. He assumes she, the one with purple hair, is in charge. It can't be the nondescript Asian woman in the black dress with her hair in bobs. Little does he know that my *hair was streaked with blue a few months earlier.*

He eases himself between us with his back to me. I reach into the thermos bag for more water and a cup while he introduces himself to her as a poet from Dover. He gives us his card, and begins a video-log of a random day in New York City. We are featured in a selfie with him.

As we talk, he is surprised to discover she is also a guest, and instead I am the host. He leaves after chatting for a little while longer.

My half hour is up. I pack up my things. She helps me fold the blanket and roll up the yoga mat.

I move to my second location near the Chelsea Mews apartment building, but I don't even get to finish setting up before the caretakers of the residence chastise me for beginning to write on the sidewalk with chalk. I move to an area in front of what seem to be the gates of a private driveway and face outward, toward the street.

What is public and what is private?

I again blow bubbles. But since I am not able to write on the sidewalk, I enact my question by trying to make eye contact with those who pass by me: "Do you have time to see?"

Not many seem to. Or would prefer not to. I smile at surprised expressions on the faces of jaded New Yorkers with their glazed eyes. No one joins me at the blanket this time, but I have seen enough. I move on after thirty minutes.

At my third location, I set up by another tree and now face a cosmetic store and macaroon shop. This time, I write in blue chalk on the sidewalk: "Do you have time to listen?"

Soon, I am joined by a white middle-aged stockbroker on his lunch break. He sits down, accepts a glass of water, and tells me that his business—a few storefronts down the block—is closing down soon.

Between sips of water, he reassures me he is okay. It's time for a new chapter anyway. He's not worried, at his age.

Just before he leaves, he turns to me and smiles. "Thanks. That's just what I needed."

At my final stop, I face the street with my back to an exercise workout facility. There is an abandoned church across from me, and behind me, another vacant storefront decorated with artwork. I write on the sidewalk: "Do you have time to be?"

A Black woman from Barbados joins me on the blanket. As had occurred with my first guest, we are silent together for a while as we blow bubbles. Surprisingly, it is not as uncomfortable as one might think.

We share stories about living in New York City. She tells me about her friends whose family dinners have become almost like board meetings, with young and old reporting schedules and commitments. They've decided to move back to Barbados, to find themselves again.

She leaves after giving me a warm hug. Another New York moment. "Thank you so much. This is what I needed."

As I am about to leave, two friends I actually know stop by. They've made it just in time to see me before I pack up for the day.

What was I doing? How did it go?

PAUSE AND REFLECT

> Echoing bell hooks's earlier words,
> This is an intervention.
> Enter that space.
> Let me meet you.
> Let us create this space to tell our stories, to interrupt, and to transform.
> Let us make spaces together that open up curiosity, wonder, and time.

- What does the sidewalk have to do with theological education? How does this story invite *you* to remember, see, listen, and be?

- If you were in this workshop, "Beauty + Purpose = Action," what would your intervention be? Where would it take place? How would you meet others in that space? Try it out!

* * *

This chapter focuses on a lesson I have been learning since an early age: *shared learning that sticks and transforms is holistic, interdisciplinary, and ongoing.* "Because by it (Christianity) I see everything else," writes C. S. Lewis.[1] We make sense of the world through the lenses we put on. They frame not only how we see but how we hear, taste, touch, smell, and feel inside. We learn theologically by integrating our present with past experiences of prayer, Scripture, worship, people, and place; sometimes our body remembers more than our mind does. This informs how we live into a future of faith with others and over time.

I share here experiences that have shaped *how I have come to know* learning as a lifelong process of theological formation and reflection, not limited to the classroom, but as a part of all of life. This was true in the South Bronx when I was a green, idealistic music teacher discovering what it meant to teach in community; in our Harlem arts gallery neighborhood group reflecting on the power of presence and hospitality; on a hot stifling summer day in East New York, Brooklyn, with family, friends, and students praying in the streets; and in a warm dormitory room in South America cooled only by a fan and open window with a student.

Formation and learning engage our whole beings and all our senses—both the physical ones and our spiritual discernment of how the Spirit moves. We cannot bear witness in this world if we have no experience of it. What I have just described is one of many ways my body has learned to listen to the city. I open myself up to be present and available. I feel the heat of the sidewalk as well as the hurt of people.

It is incarnational ministry, a translation of the gospel truth in an embodied way. It is consistent with how we have come to teach and learn together at the seminary; we do this through the Walls-Ortiz Gallery as a "third space" indoors in group exhibitions, outdoors in art workshops at the Fresh Oils Community Garden, on the street as a practice of Christian hospitality and public faith, and more recently, in building online communities. We partner with others to form a learning neighborhood, engaging with schools, libraries, parks, small businesses, community centers, churches, and more. Our approach to theological teaching and learning extends into the interstitial spaces of nonformal and informal learning, as well as in formal institutional settings. It integrates the opening of discoveries across disciplinary and demographic boundaries through time, patience, and humility. And this kind of learning takes place in the process of living life together.

* * *

I sit in front of a second-grade class in a pre-K-12 public school in the South Bronx, getting my music students ready with some singing warm-ups, and the question comes.

"Do you cook Chinese food?"

"Yes, of course."

"Really? Do you work at the place down the block, where they have fried chicken wings?"

"No. I cook at home."

Apparently, my students have never seen a Chinese person outside of the context of the kitchen behind the bulletproof plastic barrier at the American Chinese fast-food takeout down the block. I am the first one they've met who doesn't work there. This is as new for me as it is for them.

Later, my Nuyorican colleague stops me as I walk down the hallway. "Last night I was watching Kundun. *It was really good. I had no idea about the story behind the Dalai Lama."*

"Uh-huh."

"What do you think? Can you tell me more?"

"But I'm not Tibetan or Buddhist."

* * *

It was my first year with Teach for America. While my original placement was teaching secondary-school science, I ended up starting an elementary music program teaching piano and violin. The assistant principal who interviewed me saw on my résumé a decade of violin lessons and orchestra during college and asked if I was interested in teaching music instead. Thank goodness for my high school music teacher, Mrs. Koppeis, whom I quickly contacted for a crash course in teaching beginning music for elementary students.

What I wasn't prepared for were the tears, the credit-card debt, and the utter humiliation that I faced when I realized I just wasn't together enough for "inner city" kids. Everything I had done in my life prepared me to grit my teeth, get up, and start again the next day. But each of those three years, I took all ten allotted sick days, mostly for "mental health." A detached closet door propped against the wall behind my classroom door waiting for the custodian to take it away fell on my head, giving me a mild concussion, and a second grader bit my arm while I was trying to restrain him as best as I could until the dean arrived.

What did I learn? How did I learn? I learned that I was not enough on my own. And I didn't have to be. There were others with whom to learn and grow and on whom to lean.

I am eternally grateful for veteran teachers like the reading teacher Ms. Johnson and the science teacher Ms. Jenkins, who had both been there for twenty-plus years, committed to sticking with it no matter how disastrous the administrative leadership was. I learned that it was important to *stay*, to be a constant in a city experiencing never-ending change. Our students knew the Bronx and many knew Puerto Rico, as they would travel back and forth with their families, sometimes missing months of school at a time. But Ms. Johnson and Ms. Jenkins were always there, ready to help them pick up things where they had left off. These two African American elders were mainstays of the community and necessary mentors for me.

And there was a group of mostly younger teachers with whom I envisioned something more for our kids—Mr. Gutman, Ms. Johnson, Ms. Washington, and Ms. Nastri. We recruited, trained, pushed, and celebrated the achievements of young talented students in musical productions of *Changes*, *The Lion King*, and *The Wiz*. I learned to see what and who was in front of me and to draw from gifts and resources I didn't know even existed until they were revealed in conversations over meals and laughter.

Ms. Johnson, who taught first grade and had participated in choruses for years, was our singing director. Ms. Washington, who taught fourth and then eighth grade and was one of the earliest Teach for America teachers at the school, was our producer and director. Mr. Gutman was a fifth-grade teacher who had his own grunge band. He became our drummer. Ms. Nastri, the speech teacher with a distinctive Bronx Italian accent, had taken dance lessons since she was a child and became our choreographer. And there was me, Ms. Liu, the music teacher—who had taken two years of piano lessons as a child. I picked up piano lessons again, to keep up with everything I had to play—from the national anthem for assemblies to musicals, and teaching keyboard to third, fourth, and fifth graders.

I also learned a hard lesson about professionalism and the world of work. While on the School Leadership Team, trying to plan and problem-solve, I hurt a colleague mistakenly by sharing with the administration that he was uncertain about coming back the following year. What had been shared in confidence led to unintended misunderstanding and a relationship breakdown that was unfortunately not repaired by the time I left. In my earnestness to help, trying to anticipate need before it was spoken, I was left with regret and he with resentment with what I had done. I had to live in the tension that I could not please everyone, and in fact made a terrible mistake that I could not fix.

Most importantly, I learned I wasn't there to save anyone. I was learning with others how to listen first and be formed in humility and weakness. God was doing the work. I was stumbling along, getting helped up by others, and holding on to his hand for each next step forward. This was theological education in and for life. It was the formation of my MK home taken into the world, me taking on my parents' faith, curiosity, and entrepreneurial spirit. You've never done that before? You're not trained for it? No big deal. Do your best and see what God can do with (or without) you. And it translated into my work in Harlem years later.

* * *

"This is a place where healing happens. It's magical," Pastor Adrienne says.

We are a mixed group of gallery staff and neighbors: an African American neighborhood chaplain, an Asian American doctoral student and artist who studies nearby, a longtime white Harlem resident and Catholic sister, an African American photographer and gallery manager at the time, an African American neighbor and her nine-year-old daughter, and me. We are in the front room of the Walls-Ortiz Gallery, in its then-expression in a storefront on the corner of West 119th Street and Frederick Douglass Boulevard. The six-week "How Does Our Garden Grow?" community arts installation that opened in the spring of 2017 has just closed, and we are debriefing what we learned.

It begins as an idea about flowers and a garden that a nine-year-old proposes at one of our community group planning meetings. It becomes a three-part interactive exhibition-in-progress that invites healing, community, and transformation. The front room is a "garden of life," with hands-on arts activities encouraging the community to "grow" the garden roots, trunk, leaves, and fruit as well as create collaborative art pieces; the middle section is a "bridge of inspiration" with images and words of encouragement from role models displayed, complete with music from a community-selected DJ-approved playlist; and the back room is transformed into a "greenhouse lab incubator" with stations and materials to test out ideas to respond to community concerns.

As guiding questions, we ask: "What can happen when diverse neighbors come together to celebrate what is in their garden, or community, and explore how it might grow in new and unexpected ways?" with the added comment: "In a time of uncertainty and divisiveness in our city and coun-

try, we resist through the pursuit of joy and wholeness together, giving voice while listening to each other."

The installation is well received by neighbors and staff alike, and full of surprises and lessons. Art has a way with feeling, knowing, and healing.

"Remember when that father came in with his son who was so upset? The boy went to the back room to draw with one of us, and came back totally changed. He was so excited to show what he had made!" Pastor Adrienne says.

"The installation gave us the opportunity to discover gifts we didn't know were out there. The arts supply store donated a whole bunch of materials, and we got those plants from another neighbor moving out of her apartment," someone else reflects.

"This experience gave my daughter a chance to express her leadership in a way she's never done before. She was so shy before this." I am encouraged to hear our neighbor describe how she has seen her daughter grow through this project.

We pause for a moment to let it all soak in. And then one by one we continue to bear witness to the transformative power of art and the Spirit in our midst.

* * *

What is the point of having an art gallery at the seminary? City Seminary of New York's mission is to seek the peace of our city through theological education, learning as a way of life. The Walls-Ortiz Gallery serves as a third space for interaction with art, for conversation, for telling stories, for visualizing and engaging faith, and for new questions and unexpected appreciations. We bring artwork and people together, enabling them to see and experience life in a different way. We invite them to contribute their own way of understanding and seeing through guided walks and conversations through exhibitions using methods like Visual Thinking Strategies[2] or more open-ended formats, and then make art together.

American theologian Nicholas Wolterstorff suggests that "works of art are instruments and objects of action."[3] In order for action to take place—for hospitality and welcome to be enacted—art has both utilitarian and transformative roles in our teaching and learning practice. We create space for art to speak to us, for us to be transformed by the Spirit as we open ourselves to see anew. We engage critically with ourselves and others as we try to unpack the implications of what we see and its impact. Art makes possible these acts of communal resistance to the violence and trauma that pervade our everyday life, as bell hooks and Brazilian artist-theologian Yohana Junker[4] remind us. Junker's pedagogy, like ours, is very much about processing grief, loss, joy, and life through embodied creative practices.

It is through the practice of Christian hospitality as an institutional good neighbor in Harlem that we engage in public faith as well as theological reflection for and with our staff, students, and visitors. We learn with our neighbors and visitors through creative processes inspired by the ways in which artists inhabit, see, hear, and experience the world, often in prophetic witness to what is and what should be.

Seeking the flourishing of our neighborhood involves working toward the livability of the city at a local scale and promoting social change through learning at individual, group, and institutional levels.[5] The arts play a critical role in mediating the experience of living in dense, diverse urban areas by cultivating space for understanding and appreciating difference, and by helping to locate ourselves in relation to society and the city.[6] The tension with the milieu does not disappear, but instead what is brought forth is something more engaged and productive. There is potential for transformative learning and healing.

In our work, we attend to the many ways we can know and be in the world; we invite others to unlearn, and learn again how to learn. Often there are silos around creativity and emotion. Formal schooling and later higher education reinforce the notion that creative expression and exploration are a thing of childhood past. But the arts welcome us to embrace who we are, a reflection of God as Creator, as makers and gatherers, so we can respond to each other in ways that are nurturing, healing, and transformative. We discover ways to see, hear, and embody what it means to learn and care for ourselves and others. This carves out space for storytelling and listening, which moves us into a liminal space of time to be together, making possible relationships that might not otherwise exist.

Responding to how others express their experience in the world allows us to engage in common questions. Even when we don't agree.

* * *

"I think gentrification was the best thing that happened to Harlem."
What?

A local artist from a mixed racial background is sharing on an artist panel at the opening of a new exhibition. From his experience living in the neighborhood, he has felt more welcome as the demographic has changed. This he reflects in his artwork, as he explores the tension of identity and place.

As I listen, the hairs on the back of my head begin to rise. The front room of the gallery for this event is packed, and I'm sure people had different feelings about what he had just said.

A guest in the audience didn't agree. "I've lived in Harlem all my life and I can't even shop in the stores anymore. This is not the best that has happened to the community."

Oh boy. What is going to happen? Should I step in and say something? The tension is building. I hold my breath.

A third person speaks up. He also has grown up in the neighborhood. "Hey, we're not going to solve this here," he says. "Let's listen and see what the art has to show us."

Although the elephant in the room has been named, the possibility of an explosive confrontation is mediated by neighbors keeping peace in this third space, sacred to sharing and engaging with the artwork and artists. They respect that while more needs to be done, other kinds of conversations can continue outside.

* * *

Visualization of group story, Theatre of the Oppressed
NY virtual Forum Theatre workshop; photo by author
(2020)

PAUSE AND REFLECT

- Look at this image. What do you see? What makes you
  think that? How do you feel about this composition of
  seemingly random objects? What could it mean?
- Think of a situation you or someone you know is going
  through right now. If you were to use objects or images instead of words, what would the situation look like? What
  would you choose and why? How do you think it would help
  others see?

* * *

The ways we learn to use creative practices to expand our imagination and engagement come from participation in spaces like the art residency featured in the opening story and the Theatre of the Oppressed workshop that was the occasion for this photo. That workshop began when one person in our small group shared about the tensions of competing agendas for a youth leadership program and a funding organization. It grew into a five-minute interactive skit inviting "spectactors" (spectators-become-actors) to intervene and suggest possible actions. In preparation for the skit, each group member used an image to tell the story of what was happening. By stepping into and out of the story, we were able to discover different ways to see and hear potential solutions with each other; it was the creativity of the margins at work.

This assemblage was my version of the ambitious yet precarious situation facing this youth program. What was built up (the pillows) was fragile and possibly toppled down by the weightiness of its impact and the tenuousness of its support structure (held by the yarn representing people doing the work). While the core idea (the wooden stool) was solid, the other parts (funders in this case) were not.

This work moved from concept and content to the visual and the performative. It helped us translate ideas into images and our bodies in ways that opened up conversations and questions we might not otherwise have asked or addressed. Learning and expressing through the arts take us places where we can attend to the physical and spiritual reality of the city we are called to with an expanded imagination and extended vocabulary, bringing arts, faith, and place together in an integral way. And acknowledging the role of our body in learning to respond to the city is critical to ministry. This is true even as we walk the streets to pray.

* * *

"Are we there yet? It's so hot."

Josiah, my then ten-year-old, asks again. He has been grumpy and sullen since we left the cool respite of the air-conditioned subway car.

"Almost."

The roiling heat rises literally from the sidewalk. A faint echo of a breeze catches my cheek. We almost canceled because of a reluctance to embrace the weather forecast of 99-plus degrees Fahrenheit. It was hard to leave the apartment.

We wait. A bead of sweat trickles down the small of my back.

Red goes to green. Orange is replaced by white. We can go.

My daughter Immy puts her small, moist hand in mine, and we cross the street, pushing through a wall of humidity and exhaust fumes. My oldest son follows without a word.

We reach the corner, and I see what was True Holy Church City of Refuge, now turned into a construction site, surrounded by a blue-painted wood wall and metal scaffolding, a sign of change, a sign of hope. Affordable housing units are going up where the church used to stand.

We plod slowly toward the church's temporary location down the block.

The long line for the food pantry has already formed. Red and blue push-carts. Small and large plastic bags. Backpacks. There are some forty people already waiting for the 10 a.m. opening. Some in the line are young and others old. Families cluster together. Eyes watch us as we pass by, sharing the sidewalk for a moment at a time. Why are we not going to the end of the line?

The smell of heat, bodies, and anticipation follows us to the front of the line.

Pastor (now Bishop) Vivian, a tall, jovial, African American man in a blue tank top and khaki shorts, sporting a black baseball cap, is chatting with the volunteers up front and those at the head of the line.

"Pastor V—we're here!"

"Maria and the gang! You made it!"

Smiles and laughter turn to curiosity as Vivian and I hug, and he greets me and my children. We have been colleagues and friends for years.

"Are we the first?"

We linger for a while catching up. He leads us up the driveway to his office in the back of the church, where he has set up metal industrial shipping containers for food storage. In front of one are pallets of food. In front of the other is a white canopy that shields from the sun the stacks of food wait-

ing to be chosen. Yellow onions in purple plastic netting. Crates of brown eggs. Bright green lettuce, luscious red tomatoes. Colorful cans of assorted goodies. Seven or eight volunteers fill the rest of the space, busy with final preparations for their guests. We can feel the movement of bodies and anticipation in the air.

"This is Maria and her kids from the seminary I told you about. This is Michael . . . Vicky . . ."

I greet them and then find my way inside to the church sanctuary, greeted by a waft of refreshingly cool air as the air-conditioning is on high. The chairs are stacked in piles throughout the small room, which comfortably seats maybe fifty-five but is a temporary solution for their eighty-plus-member church. A small drum set and podium are in the front, and a sound system has been installed with speakers.

The kids settle in. Immy gives out handouts for the prayer walk, and the boys find seats. I head back out to greet others who are coming for the event. This has been a practice for several years now, to go to a neighborhood in each borough every year and get to know New York City at the local level, one community at a time, through written material as well as serving as neighborhood hosts. We walk the streets, visit churches and a variety of places, to listen, to learn, and to pray. We ground-truth. We calibrate with our bodies and our senses what others write or see, and what we experience of place.

We are led by the Spirit to spaces and places, inside and out, to know what it means to love our city, and thus to discover what it means to love our neighbors.

The small room fills one by one. My sister. A friend and architect who is working on our seminary renovations as well as projects in the East New York neighborhood. Seminary staff join. Unexpectedly, Philomena, a seminary graduate who lives nearby and attends a Nigerian Apostolic church in another part of the neighborhood, comes through the door. Her husband and five teenagers, who are first-timers and unsure of where their mother has brought them, join us. The room seems fuller now.

Pastor V shares about how the neighborhood has changed since he first started coming to this church at age five.

"We are on Shelter Row. There are two men's shelters, two women's shelters, and a family shelter down the block . . . we used to give out food for the pantry in prepacked bags, but we realized that the folks in the shelter

couldn't have glass jars or other items. And we have been thinking about how to give dignity to those we are serving. We've partnered with a couple of other organizations, and now it's more like a market. They sign in and come with their pushcarts and Costco bags, and choose what they want. Today we have fresh vegetables that were picked yesterday at a farm upstate. Everyone can get three dozen eggs. It's a hot day so we might not get as many as usual, but I know the regulars. Actually, I pretty much know everyone in the line. They don't all come to our church, but they call me 'pastor.'"

After Scripture reading and reflections on what we hear in the moment, someone prays, and we step out into the street to see, to listen, to walk, to smell.

How has God been here ahead of us? How are we being moved to pray?

"Is that a tour group? Who are they?"

Pastor V's wife, Bev, hesitates. "No, they are visiting."

I respond. "We're here to pray."

The woman's face relaxes. "Oh, that's good. You can pray for me . . ."

We walk for twenty minutes, pausing here and there to pray as Pastor V explains what is happening on various streets. We push through the stickiness and heat, and arrive finally at Redeemed Christian Church of God, on the edge of the neighborhood bounding Crown Heights. Opening the door lets out a welcome blast of air-conditioned coolness. Pastor Adebisi, his wife, Pastor Abby, and their granddaughters, Grace and Faithful, greet us. A feast of Nigerian food awaits us upstairs.

* * *

This "pray and break bread.NEW YORK CITY" (pbb.NYC) prayer event in East New York, Brooklyn, gives a sense of how we are learning and praying in the community. Such gatherings take what bell hooks calls the "practical wisdom about what we do and can continue to do to make the classroom a place that is life-sustaining and mind-expanding, a place of liberating mutuality where teacher and student join together to work in partnership"[7] into the streets, as we smell recycled materials sweltering in the hot sun and as we listen to those who are watching us with curiosity. Sensing the city with our bodies honors the experience of life and people in the neighborhood, and reminds us what we are doing and why we are doing it.

Pbb.NYC begins with a seminary class Mark taught early on. He arranged a Big Onion Tour of downtown Manhattan, and afterward I suggested we go for dim sum lunch in nearby Chinatown. From there, a group of students (myself included) who read Robert Linthicum's article on how to learn about and love the city began asking: "How can we pray for and love the city if we don't know anything about it?"[8] Linthicum suggests laying out a map of the city and allowing God to direct our attention to particular sites for visiting and praying. What emerges is a foundational seminary practice that pervades every possible program—from the youth seminary to our MA degree program.

We cannot pray for the city unless we know for what and for whom we are praying. Even in these pandemic times, we are out there on the street in hybrid form. Sometimes we gather together on-site; other times, our local hosts guide us in prayer as they share over Zoom and video-walk us through the community. We find ourselves praying in solidarity in our respective neighborhoods. What has become an embodied sensory experience is now translated into multiple spaces, physically on-site as well as online. We are learning how to pray with our bodies and in place.

PAUSE AND REFLECT

- Do you know where you live? Do you know your neighbors? How is God at work in the places in which you are familiar and unfamiliar?
- Walk the streets. Ground-truth the numbers you've read about the place through which you are moving and compare them with your lived experience.
- What do you see that God is doing here in your community? What don't you see? What do you want to find out more about?

* * *

"Do you need more water?"

At the end of an overseas pilgrimage, I am in a dorm room with a student. She has not been feeling well, and I stay with her while others are at dinner. We share about our various travel experiences. I realize as I listen to her how much my life experiences have shaped me, the places and the people I have encountered, and the expectations I have of myself and others. My posture has been to power through rough circumstances. No electricity? No problem. Just get a fan or sleep outside. No running water? No big deal. Just take a bucket bath.

While trying to anticipate the needs of others and manage the logistics of this trip, I see that some of my actions have been interpreted as controlling rather than addressing needs; my team and I are learning our limits, and we are realizing that ours may be very different from those of our students. While trying to make space for feelings to be expressed and choice to be inserted where possible, it is apparent that the inconveniences our group is experiencing—compounded by a lack of sleep, a rigorous itinerary, and the pace of moving with a large group—are magnified by a feeling of lack of autonomy. The result is recognizing the need to listen, reflect, and take the lessons of this experience forward.

* * *

Learning happens in community at City Seminary, and most often in the form of a cohort traveling together through their learning experience. I have shown the benefits of learning together in many of the stories I have shared. However, cohort groups should not be idealized.

They have their pros and cons. Differing and dominant personalities, the desire for self-directed learning and agency, and uneven power dynamics in an intercultural group can complicate matters. It takes intentional facilitation and difficult conversations to work this through. There may be missed learning opportunities when group members don't feel like they have the emotional bandwidth to address sensitive matters. As a doctoral student in a learning cohort, I found it easier to dig into these issues with a smaller group than with the whole group, and I imagine this may be the case for our students as well.

In an adult-learning context, as educational leadership scholar Eleanor Drago-Severson suggests, the power of a group of peers who are on a common journey with the same end goal in mind can be an energizing space, a "holding environment."[9] When there is enough support and enough challenge to push back on held assumptions, learning and change can happen.

However, adult-learning scholar Howard McClusky's theory of margins suggests that there is a delicate balance between load (burden) and power (capacity).[10] When the balance tips (as in the case of the overseas pilgrimage, and in this pandemic season), what an adult learner can handle—between child care or elder care, work, service, commuting, finances, study, etc.—may be compromised.

This has been a reality for our students in a busy city, where many are bi- or multivocational, juggling home, family, work, ministry, and school. In our Thriving in Ministry initiative, we create spaces for listening, mutual encouragement, and a power "reload" through small groups and spiritual direction retreats for pastors and ministry leaders. These groups are the context to process what one participant called "a three-dimensional journal," community that gives feedback and necessary support along the ministry journey.

In learning to address situations of stress, failure, and uncertainty, the agility and humility needed to take risks, meet frustrations, and try again are part of doing theology on the ground. To respond with resilience, we need the help not only of the Holy Spirit but also of each other. How can we think, feel, and act in a Christian way in the midst of mistakes and misunderstanding? We hope for fruits of empathy and grace. And we remember the need to get out of the way of the Spirit in order for the present moment to be illuminated by humility. We get back on our knees and pray in surrender.

Theological education for and in the city requires that we pay attention to what works and what doesn't, to the easygoing person and the one with whom we may not feel comfortable. It requires that we learn about the places we live and the people in them, because we exist in a more-than-human world. It is a place in which the whole people of God love and steward the spaces and places in which God has placed us. It requires that we sense the city and all who are in it.

In *Atando Cabos: Latinx Contributions to Theological Education*, Elizabeth Conde-Frazier writes: "The loci of our theological education are the lakes and oceans of our lives, the intersection of the practical and the theoretical as we move toward pastoral action. Our theology never comes from a blank space."[11] While she writes out of a specific context in the Latinx community, these waters of life she describes are not foreign to the doing of theology in the city street. As Revelation 22 describes this river of the "water of life" running through the city, our bodies perform public acts of prayer, worship, and knowing, discerning through the Spirit. This knowledge then takes form in new expressions in the body, the individual and the community.

We are God's "beloved," as are those we encounter each day. God is present and in the midst of the shaping influence of others. As Jesus was in the mess of ministry, so are we. And we can only grow in knowledge and practice of ministry if we do it with time for both action and reflection. How powerful it is to wrestle together with the questions of today as we face the tensions of older and younger generations making sense of politics and social justice protests. How important it is when we can walk the streets of a neighborhood together, as a mixed bag of Christians from different parts of the city, ethnic backgrounds, races, and ages, to learn, ground-truth, and pray for how God is at work. Are we willing to engage? Do you have time to listen?

* * *

"We're back in the Meat-Packing District for the last portion of the program. This time, the assignment is a seventy-two-hour intervention. Spend time exploring a particular site in the area where you would like to focus, and think about how you want to intervene. What are you asking people to do or respond to? On the last day, we will spend the day going one by one to each site as you perform your interventions."

It's another get-out-of-my-comfort-zone exercise led by residency faculty artists Ofri and Ed. My introvert self is getting a lot of practice in pushing the boundaries.

I keep thinking about the Fulton Houses, a New York City Housing Authority residence, and how—like in many NYC neighborhoods—the prosperity that has come with development projects like the High Line, a public park built on an old, unused elevated railway, has not benefited all community members equally. The Whitney Museum, the high-end retail shops, and Chelsea Market are only a few blocks away, and they have brought foot and car traffic but not necessarily jobs and opportunities for the local residents of these houses.

In conversation with Ed, I learn about the story of the "Roving Listener," an artist and community organizer from a changing neighborhood in Indianapolis whom I eventually meet and work with in our Creative Community Care virtual arts residency. He discovers the assets and gifts of the local economy—gardeners, cooks, and many more—by spending time in living rooms and on porches listening to the neighbors.

In response to the question: *Do you have time to listen?*, my answer is: Yes.

My steps lead me back down West Seventeenth Street to the Fulton Houses and "Leandra's Garden," where a mural of her is painted as the backdrop on a tall brick wall behind it. I ask a local maintenance worker on her lunch break about the story of Leandra, a young girl who once lived there. Leandra died because of an adult's drunk driving on the nearby West Side Highway, and after much activism on the part of Leandra's father, the building super, and local residents, Leandra's Law is passed. It makes driving with a child as a passenger while intoxicated a felony.

The building super shows me a mural of the three Fulton Heroes in the community room. In addition to Leandra, there is a young boy who was hit by a speeding car on the street while running out to get a ball, which led to *the installation of speed bumps on West Seventeenth Street. A third young person featured on the mural is a youth who died protecting his cousin in a domestic dispute with the cousin's boyfriend. One of the streets has been renamed in his honor.*

I listen as the local residents sitting on benches in the front courtyard share about life in the neighborhood since the High Line was built. With their permission, I record them telling stories, later edited to be played out loud as part of my intervention. These stories are shared in an audio file for others to listen to as they sit or walk through Leandra's Garden. They are also played out loud by the gate, for anyone passing who is willing to listen.

"This is the story of Leandra's Garden."

Do you have time to listen?

Impromptu crochet lesson with Mother Sandy during crocheted flower vine installation designed by Naomi Lawrence, Gate to Fresh Oils Community Garden; photo by Mark Gornik (2020)

Leading

Do you have time to be?

"I am interested."

We are choosing a chairperson for the School Leadership Team at my younger children's dual-language Mandarin public school for the upcoming year. One of the past cochairpersons, a white woman apparently used to speaking over others, continues as if I have not said anything.

I raise my hand and speak again, a little louder. "I'd like to be considered for chair this year."

She acts as if I have said nothing and continues her monologue. I look across the table at another parent, a Chinese American woman. We exchange concerned glances. The woman is now obviously ignoring me.

I speak again.

"Excuse me. I have been speaking and you are totally ignoring me. I may be new this year, but I am just as much a parent representative as you are."

"Oh, did you say something? I didn't notice."

* * *

"Is our Maria a dean? Really? I had no idea."

We are in a doctoral seminar together, and my African American classmate exclaims as if she cannot believe it, or as if I am not there. Okay, she typically speaks her mind, but really?

After class, as the burning feeling in my chest passes, I approach her.

"Remember in class just now, when you spoke about me? I was wondering why you said that. Why were you surprised that I was a dean?"

"Oh. Right."

"I was actually a bit offended by your comment. I'm not so sure I'm overreacting, but just wanted to let you know how I felt."

"Oh. I mean, I'm not questioning that you are a dean. I was just surprised. You don't seem very . . ."

"Very what?"

"I guess you're really quiet, friendly and all. I just didn't expect it."

Informal and friendly do not equal a dean? Quiet in large group settings does not equal a dean? Petite and Asian do not equal a dean?

Let me show you who and what I am as a dean.

* * *

How do these stories connect with this opening image of an impromptu crochet lesson with a neighbor on a street? The photo features the installation of a community yarn project made for the Fresh Oils Community Garden gate in Harlem during virtual yarn circles in the pandemic summer of 2020. I am there with Naomi, the local artist who designed the installation, and Sarah, a seminary colleague. Mother Sandy, a congregant of a seminary student's church, passes by. One thing leads to another. I pull out a crochet hook and yarn and show her a few stitches.

Together we are part of a larger ecology of neighbors and friends from afar who have come together to crochet flowers and leaves, building community together one stitch and hook at a time, online and in person. This installation is an effort to bring physical and relational beauty as public witness in our neighborhood, a glimpse of grace in the city. *This* is a way I lead with others. It does not require me to be loud and domineering, nor to comply with others' expectations and standards. It does mean we prioritize hospitality, action, and reflection with others. We lead together.

This chapter focuses on *leading in dynamic practice with others.* Expanding on psychologists Alice Eagly and Linda Carli's metaphor of women's leadership journeys as navigating a labyrinth,[1] I reflect on leading as dancing in and out of a spiral labyrinth with more than one center, characterizing the complexity of the journey to lead. It is not a maze with multiple entries and exits but movement into and out of centers of influence, with stops and starts, solitude and company, choreographed steps and improvisation.

Leading is a dynamic practice I have learned from my family and from generations of Asian American women leaders who have come to live into who they are as diasporic leaders, responding with their bodies to different rhythms and cadences. I have learned also from other minoritized women leaders in global theological education in Africa, Asia, and North America in my doctoral research. And this impacts the way that I lead with others at City Seminary, the Spirit choreographing our leaderful movement as a company of dancers.

PAUSE AND REFLECT

- Who and what comes to mind when *you* think of the word "lead"? "Leader"? "Leadership"?
- How often are you surprised by who you see leading formally or informally? Why?
- Close your eyes. Imagine a path before you. It may be wide or narrow. Paved or dirt. Rocky and hilly or flat. How do you see your own path and experience of leading? Is it movement along a flat, wide, smooth road? Or is it a narrow path that wraps around an increasingly steep hill leading you to a precipice? Has it changed over time and how?

* * *

Leading has become a way of being and living for me, a journey of debunking stereotypes and assumptions; it is dancing into and out of many spaces, some hostile and others welcoming. Sometimes I know the steps, and at other times I need guides and partners. To discern how to be present to the Holy Spirit, embracing the pneumatological imagination necessary for the journey, I listen first. I confessed earlier my normative impatience and tendency to move too quickly into anticipation and problem solving. I know that waiting in silence and contemplation before I move, alone or with company, is necessary. Again, I wait.

In my recent foray into making ceramic pottery with a wheel, I have been learning about the slow, quiet, painstaking process of being grounded first and centering the clay before it can be formed. There is a certain amount of physical effort and concentration needed before anything productive can happen. Leading as dancing anticipates being centered in contemplation, waiting in silence for the music, and then moving with the Spirit and the guidance of a quiet whisper. Leading as dancing pays attention to place and context, form and function, as well as creative expression and imagination. Leading as dancing opens up our imagination of what God makes possible. Yet leading is not always taking charge.

I have lived my life creatively resisting how others perceive me and their ideas of what might be broadly defined as a "leader." These stories move from perception, silence, and resistance to voice, body, and welcome. Who is there, how and where it happens, and when the Spirit moves are part of this process of leading and learning with each other.

Leading involves a relationship of influence with others. Leading involves activity that moves in a particular direction—with one leading the other or both leading toward change. Sometimes this can be mutual and reciprocal. Leading involves more than one person, action, and direction. In my mind, learning and leading are inextricably linked, and leading happens in community, in relationship with others. It is the Ephesian moment come again. *We need each other to complete the body of Christ.* It is an incarnational posture to respond to and with others.

* * *

I take off my shoes and place them alongside the other pairs of shoes and slippers lined up against the wall outside her office. She stands up to greet me as I enter, and I sit down across from her at her desk. We settle into conversation.

"Do you have a husband and children?"

"Yes."

"Oh. Then, who is taking care of your children?"

"Um . . . my husband."

"Hmm . . . I expected you to be single. I didn't think you could travel all this way if you weren't."

This is the beginning of a dissertation interview with a colleague in Southeast Asia, a woman in administrative leadership at a theological institution, someone I compose a portrait of for my research on women and leadership. Her questions tell me a lot about her.

As I listen to her story, it becomes more and more clear why she is surprised to see me. She describes the trajectory of a male counterpart who graduates from the same program at the seminary. After graduation, he moves off campus and comes back as a faculty member to teach. She also graduates but is then asked to be the resident matron of the girls' dormitory, preparing meals and hosting visitors in addition to teaching and doing research.

She sees the wives of her colleagues busily taking care of children and domestic chores, with little time to pursue their own professional careers. Years later, returning from her PhD studies abroad, she is promoted as dean. Even though she prefers to remain as a faculty member and teach, because of her qualifications and a gender quota for women leaders in the institution, she has to move into administrative leadership.

Place and context matter. I feel the privilege and burden of who I am moving through the world as an Asian North American woman with a greater degree of freedom in my own journey and growth, with enough support from my family to be on the other side of the table.

* * *

From my entrepreneurial charismatic mother to my paternal grandmother, Maa-Maa (嫲嫲), with her village wisdom, and from witty, smart female martial artists I grew up watching in Chinese historical dramas on VHS tapes, I did not lack for models of women leaders growing up; but they led within specific cultural communities. They had a bit more freedom than my colleague in Southeast Asia, but constraints were still there.

I learned early about discrimination in the wider world. In an incident in second grade, I told my teacher I was feeling hot. She, a white woman, told me to open the windows and take off my clothes. Because I was wearing only a dress with nothing else on top, I went red with embarrassment. I returned to my desk without a word, but two weeks later I awoke from a nightmare screaming that I didn't want to be naked in front of the class. When my mother asked the teacher what had happened, the teacher disregarded her, an immigrant mother, responding that as a six-year-old I had a vivid imagination. She refused to acknowledge my mother's concerns, while the latter threatened to take me to a psychologist and speak to the superintendent. When my father showed up with my mother, both of them fluent in English and now advocating with persistence, the teacher's attitude completely changed, and she apologized to me and to my parents. While I empathize with the teacher that words can be misinterpreted, her actions revealed much about the sexism, racism, and abuse of power an Asian immigrant woman like my mother had to deal with.

Teaching and leading take many forms. In a recent conversation with Chinese North American peers, my colleagues and I were talking about how our cultural heritage influences leadership. In the West, self-assertion translates into confidence and individuality, while in traditional Asian contexts, including diaspora communities, self-effacement is prized as humility and spiritual maturity. Being an Asian minority in the West means juggling and leveraging a pluralistic identity; as such, code switching is necessary. Voice and silence, presence and invisibility mean different possibilities, in the margins and at the center.

Reading through "Developing Teaching Materials and Instructional Strategies for Teaching Asian and Asian American/ Canadian Women's Theologies in North America," a document written by Asian North American women theological educators in 1999, I discovered that much of what the authors described and worked to challenge over two decades prior still remains current.[2] Asian North American women are still often the lone voices in their departments, "overworked, overburdened, and overtaxed," lacking mentoring, facing differential treatment over class (as Asian North Americans versus Asian students from the Third World) as well as racial stereotyping, mistakenly seen as "model minorities."[3] Anti-Asian racism and the black-and-white binary persist. Theological curricula based heavily on a canon of Western theological knowledge, limiting pedagogical approaches, and micro-aggressions in and outside the classroom continue in spite of such efforts to inform and reform.

Yet the women who wrote this document, and the generations of women they have mentored, persevere through the work of PANAAWTM (Pacific, Asian, North American Asian Women in Theology and Ministry). They continue to rise in leadership prominence in the wider field, notably as past presidents of the American Academy of Religion and other key organizations. However, the ways they work collaboratively led the PANAAWTM network to reflect different values. They plan and program their annual conference and other mentoring seminars with an emphasis on multiple modalities and perspectives, diverse sources of wisdom and ritual, and opportunities to dance (literally) together.

In *Attempt Great Things for God: Theological Education in the Diaspora*, Chinese American Old Testament scholar Chloe Sun explores the "interconnectedness between the local and the global, between the educational models of the East and the West, and between uniformity and diversity in culture."[4] She uses the language of servanthood rather than leadership as the goal of theological formation at Logos, the evangelical Chinese seminary in California she leads as dean. There is something in the ways that leading as serving resonates with Jesus's example.

Like these pioneers and mentors before me, I acknowledge the multiple possibilities of ways to lead. I negotiate daily how to learn and lead as an Asian American woman with a particular style of communication, addressing my own reluctance but growing openness to move toward conflict as opportunity rather than avoiding it at all costs. Perhaps because I tend to speak more informally and personally, I can be misinterpreted as being easygoing to the point of compromising on professional roles and responsibilities for personal relationship. I have learned this the hard way.

What may be well intended may not be received as such. When I have tried to act in anticipation of perceived need, which is the way I was raised as a daughter in an immigrant Chinese household, it can be taken and has been taken as making assumptions, prompting questions like, "Why didn't you ask first?" I encourage my students and colleagues to ask clarifying questions and not go up the ladder of inference immediately, a lesson I need to learn and relearn myself.

* * *

The five of us are seated around the dining table in my home. It is January 2012, and I have secured grant funding to fly three of my dissertation research participants from Indonesia, Kenya, and Ethiopia to New York. They will be speaking also at a symposium on women and leadership at the seminary, but this part of the trip is for us to meet in our collaborative inquiry group. We have had a few introductory meetings to get to know each other, and during this fourth session we get into the meat of our question and first action in response.

We have been going around the table sharing questions that we bring to the group. The question for our inquiry group that emerges explores how balancing our productive, reproductive, and community roles as women with professional expectations manifests in us, and strategies we can use to cultivate a healthy life. We are seeking practical wisdom.

After some time to reflect and journal, we go around the table sharing metaphors to describe our respective situations as women and leaders.

- *"A faucet turned on full blast"*
- *"A parched coconut tree"*
- *"A log drifting and getting bumped along as it floats down a river"*
- *"Barack and Michelle Obama smiling at a UN meeting as they shake hands with world leaders (even when they are tired and are going through the motions)"*
- *"A woman passed out in the wee hours of the night on the sofa with the light on, and with laptop and book in lap"*

These are metaphors of the physical, mental, and emotional cost of leadership. As the enormity of the collective cost of our situation sinks in, I wonder: What can possibly happen to change us in six months?

* * *

After three years of doctoral coursework in adult learning and leadership, I have come across very little mention of non-Western perspectives. I am invisible in the literature. Only once or twice, as part of a social action component of the proseminar and a critical literacy course, have we read nonwhite authors, and even when we do, they are limited to a particular topic. This can't be all there is on adult learning and leadership, perhaps all there is in English-language literature.

Fed up, I apply for a fellowship grant with my advisor, a white male but a supportive ally, to collaborate on a study funded by the dean's office at my university to examine how the program addresses diversity in teaching and learning, and the implications for faculty, students, and graduates. From critical incident questionnaires, semistructured interviews, and conversation with students and faculty, what I find is the complexity of how diversity is understood, with both students and faculty not necessarily equipped to manage difficult conversations around race and cultural diversity. Members of the learning community experience belonging and identity differently, with some feeling stronger affinity to subgroups or specific cohorts than to the larger program itself.

While students begin to question personal assumptions and cultivate a greater awareness of self and others through transformative learning practices, these do not explicitly address confronting or appreciating cultural diversity. The presence of stronger and quieter personalities, stereotypes, and assumptions, and the tension of faculty role versus student agency in directing critical conversations within an intense, fast-based doctoral program, become factors for missed or avoided opportunities. While progressive in intent, the heavily Western and male curriculum does not lend itself to leverage fully the potential to address and embrace a diversity of perspectives and sources of knowledge. My advisor tells me that until the authors' names in the handbook on our field change, this will remain the case. To me, that is simply not good enough.

As I move into my dissertation research, I am fueled by this disorienting dilemma and challenge his advice to keep things simple. I choose to do a benchmark survey, interview thirteen women in three different continents (on-site), and engage in a six-month collaborative inquiry process with four of them (on-site and over Skype). The journey is not easy with two children under the age of seven, and a third born months after I defend my proposal. But there is no time like the present to get this work done.

I fly cross-country and halfway across the world to listen to and talk with women leaders in Asia, Africa, and the United States, to learn about, describe, and embrace the ways they lead, dancing into and out of the multiple centers of a spiral labyrinth, pointing to a plurality of leadership understandings and possibilities. From South Africa to Singapore, and from Atlanta to Los Angeles, I come to know many more than these thirteen, and the opportunity to go deep and see wide brings life and transformation to my own leadership practice.

I learn about the centrality of spirituality and faith, and how each woman's identity in relationship to God is critical to how the woman leads. "Whose" these women are is more important than "who" they are. I hear about the price of leadership, its mental and internal challenges, physical cost, and cultural and systemic expectations. More than once, participants utter: "If only I were a man." The resources and support needed to counter this cost include their spirituality and personal faith journeys with God and family as well as circles of sisters, friends, and colleagues.

The portrait interviews and collaborative inquiry process become a space to hold the group of women, who become "sisters learning-within-relationships" in this collective pursuit of wisdom. Along the way, the Collaborative Inquiry (CI) group learns about time in tension, space as a gift and reminder, the impact of absence and presence on learning, the need to let go in surrender, and how learning and change take small steps. Multiple ways of knowing and being open up the importance of engaging with mind, body, and spirit; reading and listening in between the lines; and attending to how technology encourages and hinders effective communication. This life-giving journey expands my imagination and brings to light what it means to cultivate practical wisdom with colleagues, friends, and sisters on a pilgrimage.

I discover that rather than a single model of leadership to box in all these stories, these women engage in a continuum of expressions in how they have developed, practiced, and understood leadership. In fact, the challenges they have faced produce creativity, innovation, and self-efficacy as they mature in knowing themselves and others while integrating the multiple identities they hold. Critical incidents of trauma, transition, and tragedy pave the way for transformational learning and growth; surrender is not weakness or defeat but an act of strength in being reminded of one's roots, grounded in an identity as "Aslan's beloved" that allows them to be free enough to let go. One woman describes this in the form of lotus flowers growing from "muddy roots to flora." Their journeys are not unidirectional but take on multiple paths and possibilities.

These women embrace multivocal identities as assets with which to be strategic and wise in their leadership praxis, and exercise leading within a continuum of leadership possibilities. This metaphor of a spiral labyrinth with multiple centers offers a way to characterize their journeys into and out of various arenas of influence even as they walk an internal sacred journey to wisdom and acceptance. They do not limit the "center" or goal of leading to a coveted leadership position or tenure but move with flexibility toward and away from multiple possibilities, transitioning to pastoring full time or working in an accreditation association for theological education. They dance and express multiple ways of knowing as they strive to be "comfortable in their own skin" and "find their voice," carving out spaces of community and support, and calling on mentors and advocates to step up for them when the time is right.

PAUSE AND REFLECT

- According to Latinx theologian Patrick Reyes,

    a student of color is tasked with knowing multiple bibliographies. We have to know the bibliographies of our own histories, our own narratives, for the purpose of survival and passing the sacred wisdom and stories of our community down from generation to generation. And if we want to eat, we must know the bibliography of those who determine what is necessary to know. Surviving in these spaces is a call to consume knowledge as if we are starving, and this is precisely because many of us are—sometimes literally. And sometimes starving for something, someone, or God to call us to life.[5]

Reyes critiques the painful reality of students in formal theological education in its past and present forms. Sit with this for a moment. How does this speak to your own life experience? It may seem distant or dissonant, or sharply close to your own life. What does it mean for you to survive or thrive in your context? What narratives are necessary for you to know?

- Where do you locate yourself—in the centers or at the margins? How might you see the margins as a generative space for possibility?

* * *

Years after graduation, the lessons I learn from my doctoral work evolve. Learning in a cohort model. Action learning conversations. Collaborative inquiry. Action and reflection. The paradox of diversity. I continue to test the limits and constraints of theories I have learned, exploring what fostering transformative learning might look like in a learning neighborhood with an arts- and place-based approach to urban theological education. What does it mean to learn and lead from and in spaces that are not yet documented or have been deemed invisible?

In the margins of ministry, leading is pastoral care. In a North American Christian context, the words "pastoral care" may conjure up a vision of a pastor holding someone's hand at a bedside, or a couple meeting with a pastor for premarital counsel.[6]

Attending a course at the Royal Academy of Art in London, I was surprised to come across "pastoral care" in the context of house parents caring for students in primary and secondary school, and in reference to curators caring for artists, as in Lindsey Young's work for the Turner Prize in 2016 and 2018. Her main emphasis was caring for artists as they engaged in the process of nomination, selection, and articulation of their artistic process. Her pastoral care for them enabled them to do what they need to in order for their work to speak for itself.

From the Latin word *cura*, meaning "care," come both "curate"—one who is invested with the care of souls in a parish—and "curator"—one who keeps a cultural-heritage institution and is responsible for collections and interpretation. Rev. Eric Worringer, a Lutheran vicar, explores this connection of curation and pastoral identity through the theme of encountering the other.[7] While he examines this using the framework of Western thinkers Emmanuel Levinas and Dietrich Bonhoeffer, I see this worked out in the intercultural context of New York City.

As pastoral curators, we care for pastors and ministry leaders by making space for them to be themselves, to process the stresses and strains of leading and ministering in the city. We create a context where they do not always have to be "on" but can be present with each as "beloved" of God. We intentionally curate time and spaces for relationship, for encounters with God and others.

In our approach at the Walls-Ortiz Gallery, leading as pastoral curation is expressed in the Christian practice of hospitality. We care not only for our artists but also for our visitors. We welcome others into encounter and relationship with art, each other, and God incarnate in the presence of the Holy Spirit in our midst. In Korean American therapist Miyoung Yoon Hammer's interview with white ethicist Christine Pohl on the topic, Christian hospitality is articulated as a blessing for host and visitor, for both engage in vulnerability and mutuality.[8] Returning to the opening photo of this chapter, the street as well as the gallery are a third space where this hospitality, welcome, and blessing occur.

The arts play a critical role in helping us address pain and lament through pastoral care and curation. The arts enter into our lives and help us to hold and be held, to process grief when no words can help us do so. Psychologist Carl Rogers writes, "We are most fully human, most fully ourselves, when we see someone in the truth of his or her experience and are moved to respond with kindness and care."[9] In the mix of hospitality, welcome, blessing, art looking, and art making, we are able to see and respond to each other as fully human while acknowledging the presence and power of the Spirit's compassion and care.

Pastoral curating means leading with our bodies and using our senses, even those dulled by COVID-19. Not simply surviving but thriving means that we continue to stay in the city, to curate relationships and spaces to be fully present with each other in the margins and in the centers. We reframe dominant paradigms of hierarchical and individualized leadership by leaning into the power and vitality of leading as dynamic and responsive care for and with each other.

Pause and Reflect

- What comes to mind when you hear the phrase "pastoral care"? Where and when does this care happen in your context? How does it relate to thriving in ministry?
- If you lead in a family, church, ministry, or community, what does pastoral care look like for you? How have you been cared for (or not)?
- Consider music as a form through which to share your experience of thriving in ministry. If you were to develop a playlist, what songs would you choose? How long would it last?

* * *

Seminary faculty embodying "leadership" in tableau for a Ministry Fellows class; photo by a student (2012)

* * *

"You have five minutes. Since we've spent some time unpacking through the chalk talk exercise on ministry, now take it further. What does it look like to lead in ministry? Use your bodies and show with a frozen image what it means to lead."

We do as we ask our students to. Our leadership metaphor as a team at City Seminary involves more than an individual dancer; it involves a choreographed ensemble of a company moving together. Our faculty arrange themselves in various positions, connected yet articulating different aspects of what leading can mean in our midst.

As we arrange new choreography and map our steps on the streets, in our homes, and across all spaces of life, we find the "priesthood of all believers"—the young and the old and the in-between, generations present, past, and future—taking part in leading toward life and shalom in community and communion with Christ. This leading and dancing take on the potentiality of time to be and become. Being present. Being available. Being incarnational. Being together.

The image on page 113 of our core faculty from an early Ministry Fellows cohort depicts how we are responding to the questions of our times— grounded, centered, open, and expansive in our practice of leading, dancing, and welcoming. Christ remains in us as we remain in Christ. More than a decade later, the people in this photo continue the slow work of hospitality, of pastoral curating, and of dancing in unity and diversity.

* * *

At City Seminary, leading is moving in dynamic practice with the Spirit in ways that are compassionate, intentional, and hospitable. Sometimes leading with each other takes more time than we might individually prefer, but the outcome is richer and more fruitful than what we could individually accomplish. Whether carefully designed or improvised, leading and dancing as individuals and in community help us return to the idea that *theological education is for and with children, youth, young adults, parents, aunts, uncles, grandparents, families, friends, neighbors, churches, and communities*; we dance with each other in the process of formation and integration of faith and life.

* * *

"Are you here for the yarn circle? Come on in."

Clear plastic Ziploc bags filled with blue and silver crochet hooks accompanying balls of colorful acrylic yarn are stacked inside a bin, ready for the taking. Green crocheted, knit, and loomed yarn squares sewn together wrap trees lining a block in Harlem across from our community arts gallery, what we have dedicated as the Manny Ortiz Memorial, in honor of our gallery's namesake, an East Harlem Nuyorican theologian, church planter, and theological educator. These have been collected from weekly neighborhood gatherings such as this one and have also been sent in from afar.

Around the corner, between a concrete ramp leading to an underground parking garage and a neighbor's backyard with patio furniture and tomato plants, purple, blue, and pink crocheted clematis flowers adorn the entrance of a gate leading to the seminary's Fresh Oils Community Garden: they are a sign of hope and joyful resistance.

This is our context for public faith in Harlem. While it is not the buna (ቡና) ceremony that brings us together, staff and student, neighbor and visitor to Harlem, we slow down and sit together, over laughter and one crochet stitch at a time.

Our Walls-Ortiz Gallery team hosts these gatherings. New Jersey, Brownsville (Brooklyn), and Harlem; Puerto Rico, Hunts Point (Bronx), and Harlem; born and bred in Harlem; China, Atlanta, Long Island, and Chinatown (Manhattan); Ghana, the Bronx, and Harlem; Hong Kong via England, the Lower East Side (Manhattan), and Harlem—these are the respective places and cultures that have shaped us.

Catholic turned Pentecostal; Orthodox-raised, now Reformed; nondenominational, Orthodox-raised, now Reformed; United Methodist, now attending a Catholic parish; Presbyterian Church of Ghana; nondenominational as a child become "Presbycostal"—these have been formative faith experiences and expressions.

Educator, quilter, wife, minister, prayer warrior, mother, chaplain, caregiver, grandmother, artist, pastor, sister, worship leader, youth minister, brother, mentor, scholar, curator—these describe the roles we play and the gifts we bring.

Sarah, Miriam, Adrienne, Huibing, Rex, me—we are a circle within a theological learning community in the city, on a journey of becoming wise and leading together. Our stories have been woven together in intercultural spiritual formation. We have attended each other's weddings. Some of our children and grandchildren have grown up together. We have been students, and we now learn and lead each other in mutuality. The spaces for our coming together have been living rooms, sidewalks, restaurants, playgrounds, museums, churches, and gardens. We are deepening and widening a vision and experience of the Ephesian moment—the diversity of the global church walking, wrestling, leading, and dancing into and out of the centers of a labyrinth of life and ministry together.

Handwritten words to live by shared by my sister, Bethia; photo by Bethia Liu (2020)

Becoming

"Just go ahead. We'll take the Lyft when it comes."

My husband motions for me to leave first. I close the taxi door and tell the driver, "Union Square Park, north side please."

It is 3:08 p.m., and I need to get to the park to join the other speakers at the rally before it starts. Rev. Mark Ro of Joy Manhattan Church has asked me to pray a prayer of healing for the National Rally on Asian American and Pacific Islander (AAPI) Dignity and Lives, a partnership of local churches with the Asian American Christian Collaborative (AACC) in response to the March 16, 2021, murders of six Asian American women in Atlanta and the uptick of blatant racism and violence against Asian Americans during the pandemic, and in the past four years.

"Right there is fine."

The driver drops me at the east side of Sixteenth Street, and I hop out, crossing the street to the park. I see a scattering of people. It is beginning to drizzle. Two white tents have been set up by the steps, and banners are being raised behind the top of the steps where a mike stand has been placed for the speakers.

I see a few people I recognize. Pastors I know who are part of the program. Others whose names I've heard of and whom I've seen from afar. We gather under one tent.

"Thanks for coming . . ."

My family arrives just before 4 p.m. with the signs we made together around the dining table in the morning. It has been interesting and a bit difficult trying to explain what is going on to young children and teens in such a time as this.

"End Violence against Asians."

"Love Not Hate."

"Seek the Peace of the City."

Words that speak to the moment. Words that challenge. Words that hope.

This is the second time we have brought our family to a public event like this. The first was the Women's March in January of 2017. Our poster from that day is still affixed to the back of our apartment's front door. "We March for Love, Peace, and Justice."

I ask my daughter to go with me to the speakers' tent and to go up on the stage with me to pray.

"I'm afraid," she says.

"It'll be okay. Just hold my hand. You can close your eyes if you want. I need you, your courage. We'll do it together."

We wait and listen as the other speakers take their turns at the mike. Walking up the stairs. Removing their masks. Wiping the microphones. And speaking out.

Then it is our turn.

My college friend and local pastor, Reyn, introduces me and another Asian American woman who will be offering prayers of healing for the rally.

I take off my mask, hold Immy's hand, and step up to the microphone. What does it mean to be a witness? To see. To stand up. To speak out.

* * *

Wisdom shouts in the street;
    in the public square she raises her voice.
Above the noisy crowd, she calls out.

Proverbs 1:20–21 CEB

* * *

This book comes to a close with a reflection on how to *become wise in community*. Two compelling themes that draw this book and my own theological education together are the pilgrim journey and the table. As a people of God, we are pilgrims on a journey together, resting and remembering God's faithfulness as we gather around the table for meals along the way. While these practices can be done alone, they are so much richer when experienced with others.

Ugandan Catholic theologian and longtime seminary mentor Father Emmanuel Katongole challenges us to consider what it means to be on pilgrimage. He suggests that pilgrimage as "a particular form of journeying involves . . . encounter, reflection, transformation, and a readiness to be drawn into a new sense of community with those different from us."[1] In the everyday, as we make small choices and move forward in the direction God calls us, we need to be ready to receive what the Spirit brings into our lives. Only when we are attentive to the Spirit can we be transformed.

During a strategic planning meeting with my colleague Mark, my sister sent us a photo (featured here) of these words of the late French cardinal Emmanuel Célestin Suhard, as it captured what we were discussing. She had written this quotation out by hand on a Post-It to keep as words to reflect on and live by.

Suhard describes a witness as a "living mystery," one who lives in such a way "that would not make sense if God did not exist." How do we live as testimony to this miraculous relationship with God, who provides guidance, hope, and healing in the face of ambiguity, uncertainty, and violence in a complex urban world? If we reflect a plural *imago Dei* that would not make sense if God were not the center of our margins, then our families, churches, and communities take on a certain transformational quality of courage.

I return to the words of David Whyte I shared in the first chapter: "To be courageous is to seat our feelings deeply in the body and in the world: to live up to and into the necessities of relationships that often already exist, with things we find we already care deeply about: with a person, a future, a possibility in society, or with an unknown that begs us on and always has begged us on."[2]

As we wait, we are called to be present to what and who is in front of us. *Making time* for this, as the opening questions for chapters 2 to 5 ask, means *taking time to remember, to see, to listen, and to be.* Do we have the courage to spend time in encounter and reflection in order to be transformed and testify as "living mystery"? Are we willing to speak out above the crowd with our voices and lives as prophetic witness?

In this chapter, I reflect on Proverbs 31:10–31, the poem of the "virtuous woman," through an Asian American woman's lens. I explore *phronesis* as practical wisdom in the witness of my husband during this pandemic season. I then move into the impact of the living mysteries of our seminary mentors, the late Rev. Dr. Manny Ortiz, the late Professor Walls, and his wife, Dr. Ingrid Reneau-Walls.

I close with reflections on my growing civic engagement with the Asian American Pacific Islander community in New York City. *This* is what happens after the prayer rally in Union Square that opens this chapter. With my community of resistance, I am *no longer silent* in the public square. With Woman Wisdom, I cry out above the noisy crowd to say "no more," as we wait for the time that is yet to come. Becoming wise with others may mean waiting again, but I am not alone on the pilgrim journey.

* * *

> A wife of noble character who can find?
> She is worth far more than rubies.
> Her husband has full confidence in her
> and lacks nothing of value.
> She brings him good, not harm,
> all the days of her life. . . .
> Charm is deceptive, and beauty is fleeting;
> but a woman who fears the LORD is to be praised.
> (Prov. 31:10–12, 30)

At first glance, the "valiant woman" (*eshet hayil*) of Proverbs 31:10–31 appears to be the ideal woman, and even more so, the ideal Asian woman. Upholding Confucian values of filial piety and bringing honor to her family and community, being shrewd and industrious, compassionate and generous as well as capable at home and in the marketplace, she seems like everything my parents (my husband *and* my children) would want me to be. *Eshet*, translated literally from Hebrew, means both "woman" and "wife," which connotes that a woman is associated with her relationship to her husband here. Her worth appears to be measured in relationship to others.

This idea of interdependence is not necessarily a bad thing, and not unfamiliar to Asian Americans, as our collective culture bonds us to each other. We all play a role in the community structure in relationship to each other, and in performing our roles faithfully, we can bring harmony to the family, community, and society at large. Our focus on the common good is an important consideration, and we lean into the relationality of who we are as human beings living life together.

However, this "woman of worth" (*eshet hayil*) seems like Martha on steroids, busy and productive to the extreme, able to accomplish everything that needs to get done with grace and wisdom and others' admiration. *Hayil* can refer to many things: physical and military strength, social class, personal worthiness, general capability, perfection.[3] This opens up the multiple possibilities for the description of this amazing woman by the writer of Proverbs.

While the passage describes her many activities and the outcome leading to the trust and admiration of those at home and in the community, we learn that she is confident and has no fear, except for the "fear of the LORD." Her strength is seated in this "fear of the LORD," which enables her to manage the difficulties and challenges of daily life, and she even becomes a counselor-wife to her husband.

Interpreted through the eyes and life of an immigrant, an Asian American woman, and a New Yorker, where productivity, achievement, and busyness are prioritized as premium in society at large, this passage seems on the surface more suffocating and oppressive than liberating. I could see being crushed in comparison by failure and the inability to meet this standard. Yet, looking back at the stories I have shared here, I can see that the same God who is at work in the life of this virtuous woman (perhaps a composite of many!) is at work in my life. While my stories stretch beyond the domestic realm and the marketplace of a particular cultural space to much more diverse contexts, the God to whom this "virtuous woman" looks for help to manage the everyday, to make good and wise choices, is also the God who gives me confidence and courage.

While I cannot aspire to this standard of perfection, I resonate with being centered in a healthy awe of the Lord. This woman is wonderful because of whom she is related to. Her husband, *ba'al* (meaning "owner" or "lord"), trusts in her, a domestic warrior and counselor-wife, with all that belongs to him, because her heart is in the right place. But it is the Lord, not her husband, whom she fears. Her motivation and capacity come from a relationship with God, in whom she trusts. She is wise because she knows in whose hands she puts her life and everyone and everything she loves. This passage does not call me to be everything I cannot be, but to contemplate this fear of the Lord that is the beginning of wisdom (Prov. 9:10). I tell my stories as resistance and witness of this "living mystery" from whom wisdom comes, and to whom I am related.

In their introduction to *Leading Wisdom*, Korean American editors Su Yon Pak and Jung Ha Kim refer to Japanese American activist-scholar Rita Nakashima Brock's comments on wisdom: "What makes a person wise does not come from *within or without* but *betwixt and between* engaged relationships . . . it is living with 'interstitial integrity' recognizing that we are 'constituted by these complex relationships.' Our lives are imprinted with the lives of others. Wisdom is holding together what is seen and unseen in an interstitial integrity, refusing to let go of either seemingly different worlds . . . wisdom is connective, integrative, and restorative."[4] Taking the wisdom of God from the "valiant woman" in Proverbs 31 alongside Brock's argument that wisdom exists in interstitial integrity and connective spaces of relationship, the process of becoming wise involves active engagement with God and others. We are transformed by our relationships, "imprinted by the lives of others," as we recognize how God is at work in our choices and our lives. Wisdom that comes from leading with others recognizes the mutuality and importance of relationships and understands how we grow, lead, and dance because of this dynamic practice.

* * *

"Did you see a Chinese restaurant? What did it look like?"

You can't take Chinatown out of him. Wherever we travel, my husband, Tony, always looks for a sign of the familiar and the community that has formed him. Recalling the location of the opening story, we have been formed together and apart in this place that reminds us of who we are and where God calls us.

While marriages around us explode and strain, suffocated by the constraints of the pandemic, the liminal space of my home has somehow blossomed. We are far from perfect, and I am by far not the "virtuous woman" of Proverbs 31:10–31. But, by God's grace, in spite of death and loss in our family in the past year, a snowboarding accident resulting in my broken collarbone, and the reorientation of our entire family during a pandemic, we see God at work in unexpected ways.

Tony and I have entered our forties, a decade that many describe as a time of possible "midlife crisis." We have as much to look back on as to look forward to. Our oldest is finally in college, and we are in a moment of privileged choice with two younger children at home who can take care of themselves if needed. It is a time of "midlife opportunity."

While Tony's parents did what was necessary as first-generation working-class immigrants, he and his older sister Annie navigated life in Chinatown, the gangs of the 1980s, and the public school system. They went on to careers in education and social work, each pursuing two master's degrees. My sister-in-law and her family now live in New Jersey, and we remain here in the city not far from Chinatown.

Tony did not grow up in a Christian home, but he did go to an after-school program at a local church. We met in a church youth group when he was brought there by a high school friend. And fast-forward, he went into youth development and social work.

He was not formed in a home where he knew that God was directing his paths, so vocation and calling were considerations he thought about only as he got older. During the early part of his working life, he was busy taking care of the kids and working while I was in graduate school. After thirteen years of rising vertically in his career trajectory, becoming deputy director of the youth department of a major nonprofit, he decided to make a career switch.

He chose to take time and make time. Rather than supervise and manage within the organization, he wanted to spend time with people engaged in the life of the city. He took a pay cut and spent time rediscovering his first love, listening to people. He is presently working at a faith-based organization that provides funding and leadership-capacity training for Christian nonprofits across the city. In his position, he spends time connecting with pastors and ministry leaders, finding ways to support them and their organizations.

Just prior to the pandemic, he began working part time doing house calls with local youth under the auspices of a local nonprofit organization for greater personal proximity, and eventually moved into Christian counseling part time, in addition to his day job. He is leaning once more into the gifts and desires that God planted in him years ago, and embracing this season of growth. He is also dancing into a new center of a labyrinth as he lives, learns, and leads.

On the weekends and sometimes on multiple weeknights, as is his lifelong practice, he is honing his skills on the basketball court with friends he has known since childhood or picking up games with anyone who is up for it. This gift of being present and in relationship with others, intimately in counseling or physically on the court, illustrates how he has opened up his life for what the Spirit leads.

What is more, he remains close with our kids, having spent a lot of time with them when they were little and I was at graduate school or traveling for work. He remains present and attentive, listening and encouraging, joking and lifting up. Perhaps he could be described as the "virtuous husband" of Proverbs, following the call on his life in response to the fear of the Lord.

New Testament scholar Wayne Meeks writes about the "shaping of a Christian phronesis, a practical moral reasoning that is conformed to

[Christ's] death in hope of his resurrection."⁵ Latino scholar Eldin Villafañe argues further that this notion of Christian thinking is not only about rational thought but includes "emotion and attitudes as well as the ensuing lifestyle that proceeds from them."⁶ Taking these together, the practical wisdom that Tony is cultivating and living out comes from theological formation in his thinking, feelings, and action. Small acts of obedience shape and transform him as he waits patiently for God's direction.

From this witness, a mystery to me as I am inherently impatient, I have learned what it means to be still, to pray, and to wait. His approach to life is to consider his options methodically before testing them out, while I learn through experience, trial and error. We have discovered what it means to bring together two very different people, one eager to act and the other ready to wait, to become wise in community. Waiting together in order to be wise. We fear the Lord not as individuals but as a family. We are on a journey of phronesis of discernment as we parent, minister, and do life together.

* * *

The beginning of wisdom is to call things by their right names
(名不正,則言不順).
—*Analects of Confucius* (論語)

* * *

As I have acknowledged my elders in the Asian American community, it is only appropriate to name others at the table who have made this pilgrim journey transformative: the late Reverend Dr. Manuel Ortiz, affectionately known in our community as "Manny"; the late Professor Andrew Walls; and his wife, Dr. Ingrid Reneau-Walls. They have been mentors, guides, and recognized by name at the Walls-Ortiz Gallery.

I mentioned earlier the Manny Ortiz Memorial yarn bomb, a series of trees covered with crocheted, knitted, and loomed yarn squares. The fact that his memorial was made by many hands from our community emphasizes his love for bringing people together in relationship. Manny was a leader in our learning community, serving as board chair of the seminary as well as advisor and teacher. His memorial joins two other memorials in our Harlem community, a statue of Harriet Tubman to the north and a statue of Frederick Douglass to the south.

One thing I remember from the memorial service celebrating his legacy was something his son shared. Manny was a busy man, planting churches and schools, teaching and caring for the broader Latino theological community. But he always had time for his family. While I cannot remember his son's exact words, I heard in them that his father was present and available, even in the midst of his many commitments as leader, theologian, and pastor.

Even now, we are blessed by the legacy of theological formation that happened in Manny's home. His daughter, Debbie, continues to host our students when they come on pilgrimage to Philadelphia. She has come up to New York City to participate in our annual women and leadership symposium. His granddaughters have also been up to the gallery to visit, celebrating his life at the opening of the Manny Ortiz Memorial.

The late Professor Andrew F. Walls, who recently died at the age of ninety-one, also left a legacy imprint on us. A grandfather to us all, Professor Walls was a world-renowned missiologist and historian who founded the Centre for the Study of Christianity in Edinburgh, Scotland. His thinking on the Ephesian moment—addressing our diverse urban moment as foreshadowed by the biblical city of Ephesus and the necessity for the church to recognize that no one part of the body of Christ is complete, that we need each other—has been pivotal to how we frame our work.

In spite of a busy schedule of teaching internationally—moving from Aberdeen to Liverpool to Ghana and then to the Philippines with his wife, Ingrid—Professor Walls continued to be present in our lives at the seminary, whether he was speaking on "conversion" and inviting us back into the story of the early church and how cultures turned to the gospel in their own ways or was sitting down with one of us in conversation. He once spent two hours helping me identify candidates for my dissertation research work on women in global Christian theological education, many of them his former students.

At the final colloquium session of our inaugural MA cohort, held on Zoom because of the pandemic, Professor Walls gave an important charge to the group as they prepared to close this chapter and begin a new one. This was one of the last times he was to speak to our community. Mark, our seminary director, then invited Ingrid to speak. She shared a powerful reflection on our encounter with death and loss. This was during the height of the pandemic in New York City. Hospitals were full to the brim, and mobile cooling units housed bodies waiting to be moved. Everyone knew someone who was infected or had experienced a loss.

Ingrid asked, "How do you hold onto peace in the midst of such horrors, the death, and the loss? What is good about death? The Lord Jesus proclaims his death, not his resurrection, until he comes. Why?"

Ingrid shared how she and Professor Walls had been taking communion daily together as part of their prayer time. She reflected on how the Scripture around communion allows us to fully enter into a "more real experience of in-betweenness between victory over the cross and the time to come." During the pandemic, described by some as a "portal" or a "liminal space," we are able to pause our hurried lives, previously too preoccupied perhaps to notice and experience this "in-betweenness." During this moment of pause, we are reminded again that we literally *need each other* to complete this work of the church. Death and life mark how and in whom we hope.

So, we return to a liminal space in the process of being formed in and over time—both *chronos* in its sequential sense and *kairos* as the opportune moment. The pilgrim journey we walk requires that we pause around the table and get on our knees to pray a prayer of lament and healing, an invitation to self-reflection as well as encounter, with self, God, and others. In our waiting together, in this process of becoming wise along the journey, we discern the dance and movement of the Spirit. We begin again. Re-create and make us new.

PAUSE AND REFLECT

- How are we a people of testimony, and how do we engage in the joy-work of sharing our lives?
- How do we become a "living mystery" that would not make sense if God did not exist?
- How are you living in God's peace in the groaning and aching of a broken world, in the wake of pandemic and protest, in compassionate care of creation?

* * *

Wisdom and institutions—what does it mean to be in community, to belong in the crowd, to do the work together? How do we interrogate existing institutions and logics that are irrelevant or actually destructive to the work that needs to be done? Are we willing to learn to unlearn the ways in which we have participated in the malformation of families and of friendships, and in our learning and our leading? In this journey of theological formation, we hold a heavy responsibility as pastors, lay leaders, board members, administrators, parents, brothers, and sisters. We have the opportunity to see and hear and engage anew a vision of theological education that is not for the one but for the many, that is for the crowd around Jesus, as Willie Jennings writes. This is a vision of the journey and the table that means teaching, as Elizabeth Conde-Frazier writes, a priesthood of all believers, for *kōinōnia*.

Transformative learning, the changing of our hearts and beings, begins with an encounter or disorientation, an acknowledgment of sin, whether intentional or not. But the next step of reflection is important, and the one after that, and the one after that. Small steps of obedience lead to change. Becoming is the process, and wisdom is the goal, but it exists in the "interstitial integrity" of relationship, in liminality. As Asian American theologian Sang Lee proposes, there is creative potential in the liminal space, the in-between, the not-yet; in this moment of waiting in between the times as the church, as families, as communities, and as theological educators, *how* we spend our time matters.

What does this have to do with the church in the world, living in the present yet hoping in the future, grounded in a historical past and reality of Jesus's death and resurrection? What does the Asian American community—yes, people like me—have to offer in the consideration of how theological education moves forward into a future in North America and at large? We have an opportunity to move from a dominant rhetoric and systems emphasis on the center and the margins. We can embrace a notion that there are multiple centers of influence in the church and in the world, and these are spaces where knowledge and wisdom reside, in the building of bridges across cultures and places.

What does love mean in the Asian reality of long-suffering, lament, patience, endurance, and persistence? What does it mean across generations? As a next generation Asian American growing up in the West, I reinterpret my parents' generation and their passion to serve with their whole heart, minds, and lives. I expand my imagination to see that there is a possibility for both-and, and we are not limited or constrained to either-or. I press into the tension that exists in being like Ruth, of embracing an anchored identity as part of the broader, beautifully diverse *imago Dei*.

Over the past several months, I have become active with a coalition of Asian American Pacific Islander (AAPI) Christians in New York City in the public square. This loose network, formed in 2021 after the murders of the Asian American women in Atlanta mentioned in the opening story, has made space for people like me to wait and lead together with purpose. We have met with elected officials; have been present at the Mayor's Interfaith Leaders Network and other civic entities, speaking out against gun violence or anti-Asian hate; have hosted a prayer rally for public lament; and have coordinated a prayer walk through Chinatown as part of a movement for Black-Asian solidarity.

I had the opportunity to interview a number of core members as I documented the coalition's work for the past year in a digital story map. It was humbling to see how God has brought individuals together in a "leaderful" movement, one that makes space for each of us to use our particular gifts and areas of influence to speak up and speak out for and with our community. I have not seen this kind of engagement from the AAPI Christian community in New York City in my lifetime. I hope that as we wait for true peace and justice to come, we can continue to be courageous and prophetic, out of our collective fear of the Lord, and live into the wisdom of relationship, impacting the city beyond our own ethnic community.

So, what hope do we have for the future of urban theological formation and education? In this work of excavation, as a curator, I have mined the artifacts of this life built on street corners, in coffee shops, and in church basements. This book is a curation of memories, artifacts, and experiences that has made my own journey and that of City Seminary one that continues to be interrogated and celebrated, in the act and fact of its existence. The images, stories, reflections, and provocations are part and parcel of a curated exhibition and a pedagogy of hope, joy, and resistance.

At City Seminary, we journey as pilgrims together—taking on daily the slow, prayerful, and persistent work of building intercultural relationships inside and outside of the church. We do the deep, hard work of living out God's peace in our neighborhoods. This can feel like precarious and delicate work at times. There is pain, and there can be misunderstanding. But there are also unexpected moments of grace, joy, and light. Yes, light that you don't see until it surprises you.

The Ephesian moment of the diversity of peoples—from a range of cultures, generations, Christian traditions, communities, professional and vocational experiences—coming together as the church in the city is not simply a potluck of different dishes laid on the table together. Praying and breaking bread—as we do in neighborhood after neighborhood each year—means taking time, making the effort, and opening ourselves to new experiences, and indeed, flavors. It means letting the different dishes come together as a shared feast.

Going to each other's homes and communities. Seeing and hearing each other's pain and joy. Walking the streets. Feeling the ground beneath our feet. Smelling the spices of local restaurants and the stench of neglected places. Ground-truthing what is written with what is seen and experienced. We are sensing the city, the people and places, with each other. These days it may sometimes be over Zoom, but it will not always be so. It is living the stories together. It is becoming wise together, a process that cannot be replaced by a book. We learn in community, leading and being led by each other, in our home, in the city.

Theological formation happens in the formal, informal, and nonformal interstitial spaces of life. Such theological formation is not solely for the individual but is embedded in the life of community, both planned and spontaneous. This process is not something done alone. My story is my own, but it is intertwined with the stories of others who are walking this journey with me.

The story that began this book was one of waiting. As a child and still now as an adult, waiting was and is an ambivalent experience for me. I am naturally impatient, and God knows this is the particular area of growth on which I will always need to work. Leaning into a healthy theology of waiting, I am being formed in a process of asking questions and cultivating a posture of attentiveness, as British theologian Rowan Williams suggests in his book *Being Disciples*: waiting, being present, and paying attention for glimpses of grace, movements of the Spirit, like a birdwatcher. Praying and being patient.

Theological education begins with the people of God coming to know who they are, whose they are, and where they are from, and then moving on to understand, practice, and embody faithful Christian living in the image of God while drawing others into this reality. It begins with embracing a vision of the living mystery of the unity and diversity of the church, and recognizing there may be an entire ecosystem of theological education paradigms we are moving toward that we have not yet imagined. And in the context of changing times and politics, this work becomes more and more important to serve those who seek relevant and responsive theological education for the practice of ministry. The end, or *telos*, of this work is *the flourishing of God's people and world, the reconciliation of brokenness, and glimpses of grace and wholeness in families, churches, and communities across the world.*

Welcome. Join in the joy-work.

* * *

At the AACC rally this chapter opened with, Rev. Richard Lee—AACC staff, a pastor, global director of public engagement at International Justice Mission, and a friend of mine for over two decades—charges us with this: "Lift up your heads and get in good trouble. Take up space. This is our home."

I take up space. This is my prayer that I shouted out a bit too loudly into the microphone, according to my children, to the city streets at the AAPI rally in March 2021. It still holds today.

> *O gracious and mighty God—*
> *you love and care for us*
> *You call us "beloved"*
> *You invite us into relationship with you*
> *So that as you dwell in us*
> *we might dwell in you*
>
> *On this Palm Sunday*
> *You remind us how you entered into Jerusalem on a donkey*
> *On your journey to the cross*
> *In humility*
> *In suffering*
> *In solidarity*
> *With your creation*
> *Knowing that it is not hate and violence*
> *But your love and sacrifice*
> *That breaks the power of sin*
>
> *We pray now for healing*
> *For you to be the balm of Gilead*

BECOMING

To soothe us in our suffering
To bring justice and healing
To bring peace and wholeness
To bring comfort to those who have lost loved ones

To welcome those who have been rejected, mocked, or ignored
For those who have been called names or told to go home, we know
you are our home and yet this is the place you have called us to
For those who have been bruised, beaten, and battered
For our elders, our children, and all those in between
We ask for physical, mental, emotional, spiritual, and social healing
Protect us against bitterness and resentment
Open our hearts
Soften our jadedness
Cause us to have hope in your healing grace
In the power of the Cross
In the power of your Resurrection

We are all made in your image
Your dignity
Your divinity
Is reflected in us
And we pray that we recognize that in each other
Expand our imagination
In the midst of our pain
In the midst of our anger
In the midst of our numbness

We seek your healing
Which is only possible
When you—the God of the universe who cares and knows about
each hair on our head—enter in
And dwell in our hearts and our lives

In faith and obedience
Let us become and live out your peace, your shalom

CHAPTER 6

In our hearts
In our families
In our churches
In our workplaces
In our communities
In our cities
In our nation
And indeed, in our world

God, grant us your strength to do what we cannot otherwise do on our own
Remind us daily
That the healing that we seek and expect
Comes from you

This healing is not only for ourselves
As Asian Americans and Pacific Islanders
As friends and supporters
But for us all

For those who do not understand or see us
For those who do not care or hear us
For you are a God of miracles
And you will break the bonds of sin
And surprise us
For your love is bigger and more abundant than we can
comprehend

For Psalm 42 reminds us

"Deep calls to deep
in the roar of your waterfalls;
all your waves and breakers
have swept over me.

BECOMING

By day the Lord directs his love,
at night his song is with me—
a prayer to the God of my life
. . . . .
Why, my soul, are you downcast?
Why so disturbed within me?
Put your hope in God,
for I will yet praise him,
my Savior and my God."

We will yet praise and put our hope in you
Our God who brings healing and life.
Amen

For Further Thought

While much more can be said and read about what I have mentioned in this short book, what I encourage rather is taking into your mind, body, and spirit a range of possibilities that emerge from these stories and provocations. How are you making sense of all this, and what connections and applications do you see in your own work and communities? I welcome you to explore this with family, friends, colleagues, neighbors, or even your congregation.

Go on this journey together.

You may have tried out an activity or two from suggestions in each chapter, and now you are wondering what is next. Here are several suggestions for further thought and action, a few more opportunities to take an active stance in this journey between the times. . . . Consider when, where, with whom, why, and which of these you'd like to try out first.

AT HOME

Fold a piece of paper in half. Fold it again in half. Open it up. Write about four moments in your life in which God has met you. Use words or phrases, bullet points or whole sentences.

Where were you? With whom were you? What happened? What surprised you? How have you changed? What questions came out of this experience? What thread do you see guiding you through these four moments?

Share these stories with someone. Listen to someone else's stories.

Consider the places or contexts in which you and your conversation partner were formed theologically as you reflect on what aspects are unique and what you share in common. How can this inform your understanding of what theological education is and what it is for?

Now, collect images or objects in your home. Imagine you are curating a traveling art exhibition and only have room for ten items. What would they be? How do they tell your story? What themes emerge from this collection?

On the Street

In chapter 4, I begin with a story about beauty + purpose = action. I asked:

Do you have time to remember?

Do you have time to see?

Do you have time to listen?

Do you have time to be?

As you consider these four questions, try out some of these exercises. Where do they lead you? How do you see God forming you and reframing the way you see and move about the world?

Explore the neighborhood with your cell phones, cameras, iPads, or similar. Document how different people, buildings, and animals have (been) adapted in this environment. Take photos or videos as you move through space at a different pace.

Find a place to sit for at least thirty minutes. Don't take out your phone. Don't take out a journal or book or something to keep busy. Just look around.

Where do your eyes take you? Do you follow people walking by? What do you see above you? Around you? Close your eyes.

Bring a friend to help keep watch if you don't feel safe closing your eyes in public on your own. Why don't you feel safe? Pay attention to your surroundings, but also pay attention to your emotions. How do they affect your heightened sense of presence? Or not?

How do you see differently as a result of this exercise? How do you experience the neighborhood from a different vantage point?

At the Park

The next time you have the opportunity to take a walk outside, slow down your pace and look at who is around you.

What do you see?

Who is not here?

Who is here?

For Further Thought

In the Museum

With whom do you go?

How do you "see" together?

Where can you invite conversation?

Walk around the museum's exhibits and use a mobile phone, camera, iPad, or similar to document what you see together and apart.

With a Friend or More

How do you walk together?

How are you changed differently by each other when there are more than two of you?

Do you dare become friends? How can you become known and belong with each other in an entirely different way?

By Yourself or in Conversation with Others

If you have time to dip into some other places to explore theological formation in an embodied way, in the city or wherever you find yourself, here are a few resources to push you outside of the box:

Lupi, Georgia, and Stefanie Posavec. *Dear Data: A Friendship in 52 Weeks of Postcards*. New York: Princeton Architectural Press, 2016.

Shalom, Todd. *Prompts for Participatory Walks*. Istanbul: Elastic City, 2019.

FOR FURTHER THOUGHT

The Pedagogical Impulse: Research-creation at the intersections between social practice and pedagogy. https://thepedagogicalimpulse.com/ (in particular, check out the Instant Class Kit).

Walker, Rob. *The Art of Noticing: 131 Ways to Spark Creativity, Find Inspiration, and Discover Joy in Everyday Life.* New York: Knopf, 2019.

Or explore the creative work of Elizabeth Conde-Frazier, Mai-Anh Le Tran, Lynne Westfield, and others.

Notes

Chapter 1

1. Yong explores this further in his book in this same Theological Education between the Times series, *Renewing the Church by the Spirit: Theological Education after Pentecost* (Grand Rapids: Eerdmans, 2020).

2. Amos Yong, "Theological Education after Pentecost," Oikonomia Network, accessed October 19, 2022, https://oikonomianetwork.org /2021/02/theological-education-after-pentecost/.

3. There have been substantial investment and interest in the philanthropic world and accrediting agencies on innovation in educational approaches and financial models. This book series itself is part of documenting this work.

4. Acts 2:2–4 NIV. Unless otherwise indicated, all Scripture quotations in this book come from the New International Version (2011).

5. See bell hooks's catalytic essay, "Choosing the Margin as a Space of Radical Openness," in *Yearnings: Race, Gender, and Cultural Politics* (New York: Routledge, 1989), 203–9.

6. hooks, "Choosing the Margin," 203.

7. In Andrew F. Walls, "The Ephesian Moment," in *The Cross-Cultural Process in Christian History* (Maryknoll, NY: Orbis, 2002), 72–81.

8. If you are interested in exploring further, read more about autoethnography and collaborative autoethnography in the work of Heewon Chang.

9. Heather Walton, *Not Eden: Spiritual Life Writing for This World* (London: SCM, 2015). Walton expands on this practice in *Writing Methods as Theological Reflection* (London: SCM, 2014).

10. David Matzko McCarthy, *The Good Life: Genuine Christianity for the Middle Class* (Grand Rapids: Brazos, 2004).

11. hooks, "Choosing the Margin," 209.

12. David Whyte, *Consolations* (Langley, WA: Many Rivers, 2014).

Chapter 2

1. More information about this can be found in Paul Woods, ed., *Shaping Christianity in Greater China: Indigenous Christians in Focus* (Eugene, OR: Wipf & Stock, 2018).

2. Deborah Hearn Gin, "Ruth: Identity and Leadership from Multivocal Spaces," in *Mirrored Reflections: Reframing Biblical Characters*, ed. Young Lee Hertig and Chloe Sun (Eugene, OR: Wipf & Stock, 2010), 57–71.

3. Justo González, *The History of Theological Education* (Nashville: Abingdon, 2015).

Chapter 3

1. Augustine, *Sermon Denis* 16.1.

2. Clive Staples Lewis, *The Four Loves* (New York: Harcourt Brace, 1960), xx.

3. See http://www.sspeterandpaul.us/announcements/nostvincent strambicollectioninjunemissionco-opvisitfromyarumalmissioners. Accessed November 1, 2020.

4. David Whyte, *Consolations* (Langley, WA: Many Rivers, 2014), 71.

5. Chorus from song "Lord You're So Good," written by Samuel Nwachukwu, https://www.last.fm/music/CalledOut+Music/_/Lord+You%27re+so+Good/+lyrics, accessed November 20, 2022.

Chapter 4

1. C. S. Lewis, "Is Theology Poetry?" in *The Weight of Glory* (New York: Macmillan, 1949).

2. Find more about Visual Thinking Strategies as a method of build-

ing visual literacy and making space for diverse perspectives to be heard at https://vtshome.org/.

3. Nicholas Wolterstorff, *Art in Action: Towards a Christian Aesthetic* (Grand Rapids: Eerdmans, 1987).

4. Yohana Junker, "Art as a Way of Feeling, Knowing, and Healing," *Wabash Blog*, December 2021, https://www.wabashcenter.wabash.edu /2021/12/art-as-a-way-of-feeling-knowing-and-healing/.

5. This argument builds on work with Carrie Myers and Sarah Gerth van den Berg in previous collaborations presented at the Society of Vineyard Scholars in Media, PA (2015) and the PASCAL Observatory Annual Conference in Pretoria, South Africa (2017).

6. Peter Jarvis, *Globalization, Lifelong Learning, and the Learning Society* (New York: Routledge, 2007).

7. bell hooks, *Teaching Community: A Pedagogy of Hope* (Abingdon, UK: Routledge, 2003), xv.

8. Robert Linthicum, "Learning How to Love Your City," *Together*, July–September 1991, 22.

9. Eleanor Drago-Severson, *Helping Educators Grow: Strategies and Practices for Leadership* (Cambridge, MA: Harvard Education Press, 2012).

10. Howard McClusky, "The Course of the Adult Life Span," in *Psychology of Adults*, ed. W. C. Hallenbeck (Chicago: Adult Education Association of the USA, 1963).

11. Her book is also in the Theological Education between the Times series. Elizabeth Conde-Frazier, *Atando Cabos: Latinx Contributions to Theological Education* (Grand Rapids: Eerdmans, 2021), 72.

Chapter 5

1. I refer to the preface of Alice Eagly and Linda Carli's *Through the Labyrinth: The Truth about How Women Become Leaders* (Cambridge, MA: Harvard Business Review Press, 2007), ix–x.

2. Rita Nakashima Brock et al., "Developing Teaching Materials and Instructional Strategies for Teaching Asian and Asian American/Canadian Women's Theologies in North America," Pacific, Asian, North

American Asian Women in Theology and Ministry, accessed October 25, 2022, http://www.panaawtm.org/presentations-papers-research/.

3. Brock, "Developing Teaching Materials," 31.

4. Chloe Sun, *Attempt Great Things for God: Theological Education in the Diaspora* (Grand Rapids: Eerdmans, 2020).

5. Patrick Reyes, *Nobody Cries When We Die: God, Community, and Surviving to Adulthood* (Nashville: Chalice, 2018), 50–51.

6. Mike Calvert expands further in his article, "From 'Pastoral Care' to 'Care': Meanings and Practices," *Pastoral Care in Education* 27 (2009): 267–77.

7. Eric Worringer, "Encountering the Other: Curation and Pastoral Identity," Society for the Arts in Religious and Theological Studies, accessed October 25, 2022, http://www.societyarts.org/encountering-the-other-curation-and-pastoral-identity.html#.

8. Miyoung Yoon Hammer and Christine Pohl, "Restoring Hospitality: A Blessing for Visitor and Host," Fuller Studio, accessed October 25, 2022, https://fullerstudio.fuller.edu/restoring-hospitality-blessing-visitor-host/.

9. Cited in Reyes, *Nobody Cries When We Die*, 18.

Chapter 6

1. Emmanuel Katongole in an interview with Andy Crouch, "From Tower-Dwellers to Travelers," *Christianity Today*, January 24, 2013, http://www.christianitytoday.com/ct/2007/july/9.34.html.

2. David Whyte, *Consolations* (Langley, WA: Many Rivers, 2014).

3. Roger N. Whybray, *The Book of Proverbs: A Survey of Modern Study* (New York: Brill, 1995).

4. Su Yon Pak and Jung Ha Kim, eds., *Leading Wisdom: Asian and Asian North American Women Leaders* (Louisville: Westminster John Knox, 2017), 7–8.

5. Wayne A. Meeks, "The Man from Heaven in Paul's Letter to the Philippians," in *The Future of Early Christianity: Essays in Honor of Helmut Koester*, ed. Birgir Pearson (Minneapolis: Fortress, 1991), 333.

6. Eldin Villafañe, *Beyond Cheap Grace: A Call to Radical Discipleship, Incarnation, and Justice* (Grand Rapids: Eerdmans, 2006), 8.